Pfaueninsel, Berlin

**Text
Michael Seiler**

**Photographien/Photographs
Stefan Koppelkamm**

Wasmuth

Herausgeber/Editor: Axel Menges

Mitherausgeber dieses Bandes:
Verwaltung der Staatlichen Schlösser und Gärten
Berlin
Co-editor of this volume:
Verwaltung der Staatlichen Schlösser und Gärten
Berlin

© 1993 Ernst Wasmuth Verlag, Tübingen/Berlin
ISBN 3-8030-2713-6

Englische Übersetzung/English translation:
Christina Rathgeber
Gestaltung/Design: Axel Menges

Printed in Korea.

Inhalt/Contents

Andeutungen über die Pfaueninsel
(Martin Sperlich gewidmet)

Gleich einem Delphin, der angesichts der Landenge bei Sacrow mit hochgereckter Schwanzflosse auf seinem Weg nach Potsdam innehält, so erscheint dem phantasievollen Betrachter die 67 ha[1] große Pfaueninsel auf der Landkarte. Dem auf dem Schiff Vorüberfahrenden verwehrt die Insel mit hohen Uferbäumen den Einblick in ihr Wesen. Nur die theaterhaften weißen Fassaden von Schloß und Meierei zeigen sich lockend am Ufer, während Kastellanhaus, Fährhaus, Fregattenhafen und Jagdschirm unter Laubdächern entdeckt werden wollen. Wenn dann noch ein vielstimmiges, klagendes Rufen der Pfauen im Inneren der Insel auf- und abebbt, ist die Atmosphäre des geheimnisvoll Exotischen vollkommen.

Von Martin Sperlich stammt der den Kern treffende Satz: »Das Körpergefühl der eigenen Bewegung ist der Hauptsinn für das Verstehen des Raumkunstwerkes Garten.«[2] Eine umfassende oder gar gründliche Beschreibung eines derartigen Gesamtkunstwerks, das durch eigene Bewegung erfahren werden will und Mehrdeutigkeit zu seinen künstlerischen Mitteln rechnet, ist vernünftigerweise nicht erreichbar. Ich muß also versuchen, durch Andeutungen, ich greife damit bewußt das von Fürst Pückler so überaus passend gewählte Wort auf, dem Interessierten eine charakteristische Skizze zu vermitteln, die sich ihm jedoch erst durch einen Besuch der Insel zu einem Ganzen runden kann.

An den Genius loci anknüpfend, wurde das Gesamtkunstwerk Pfaueninsel in zwei Stilphasen entwickelt. In der letzten Phase wurde durch die künstlerische Kraft des genialen Landschaftsgärtners Peter Joseph Lenné das Vorausgegangene adaptiert und seine Idee in einem neuen, viel dichteren und subtileren Bild vollendet. Die erste Phase begann mit dem Jahr 1793 und gehört dem sentimentalen Landschaftsgarten an. Ihre Gestaltung wurde durch die Vertraute und Jugendgeliebte des preußischen Königs Friedrich Wilhelm II., die Gräfin Lichtenau, den Monarchen selber und den Hofgärtner Johann August Eyserbeck bestimmt. In der darauffolgenden Zeit, von 1805 bis 1816, war die Insel »ferme ornée«.[3] Davon blieben kaum Spuren, aber dieser transitorische Zustand war für das folgende, die Insel gültig prägende gartenkünstlerische Bild von ausschlaggebender Bedeutung, gleichsam die Verpuppung vor dem Ausschlüpfen des Schmetterlings. In der zweiten Phase, der des reifen Landschaftsgartens, gestaltete Lenné im Verein mit Joachim Anton Ferdinand Fintelmann von 1816 bis 1834 die Pfaueninsel tiefgreifend neu, ohne jedoch das Vorhergehende gänzlich auszulöschen. Er führte die Themen der ersten Phase in vielfältigen, künstlerisch sensibleren Variationen fort. Dabei wurde nicht ein allumfassender Entwurf umgesetzt, sondern die künstlerische Phantasie inspirierte sich während des langen Gestaltungsprozesses an dem bereits Geschaffenen und verdichtete und verfeinerte fortschreitend das durch die Form der Insel vorgegebene Bild. Vorzüglich hat Fürst Pückler diese von der Architektur abweichende Arbeitsweise beschrieben.[4] Anders als in der ersten Phase wurde nun auch ein dem Landschaftsgärtner zumindest ebenbürtiger Architekt beteiligt, Karl Friedrich Schinkel. Das Ganze wäre naiv geblieben ohne die Weiterarbeit der beiden nachfolgenden großen Künstler. Ihr Wirken steigert das Vorhergehende und wertet es auf, ohne es zu vernichten. Kein architektonisches Objekt der Insel hätte für sich genommen die Ausstrahlung und Bedeutung, die es als Teil und im Gesamtbild der Insel gewinnt. Der äußerst komplex komponierte Garten Lennés weist jedem Gebäude seinen Platz an und ist die sinnstiftende Kraft, die alles im Innersten zusammenhält.

Bronzezeitliche und slawische Siedlungsfunde bezeugen, daß die Menschen jener Zeit die Vorteile der Insel zu schätzen wußten. Danach blieb die Insel über Jahrhunderte romantische Wildnis, die sich hauptsächlich über den Wasserweg erschloß. Erst unter dem Großen Kurfürsten trat sie, zuerst ganz bescheiden, in das Licht der Geschichte. 1683 wurde auf der Westspitze in der Nähe des heutigen Schlosses ein Kaninchenhegerhaus errichtet, und man zog dort jährlich etwa 800 dieser Tiere. Der bisherige Name der Insel, »Pfauenwerder«[5], wandelte sich zu »Kaninchenwerder«. Schon das antike Rom kannte Einhegungen, genannt Leporarien, in denen man Kaninchen hielt, eine Tradition, die sich in italienischen Renaissance- und Barockgärten fortsetzte. Dort lebten die Tiere oft auf kleinen Inseln. Bekanntestes Beispiel ist die Kanincheninsel im Park von Valsanzibio. Möglicherweise hat sich der Große Kurfürst dadurch anregen lassen, die abgelegene Insel in solcher Weise zu nutzen. Aber schon 1685 mußten die Langohren höheren Zwecken weichen, nur ihr Name blieb noch mehr als ein Jahrhundert an der Insel haften. Der Große Kurfürst schenkte seinem Kammerherrn, dem Chemiker und Glastechnologen Johann Kunckel, die Insel. Dieser richtete dort ein Geheimlaboratorium ein, in dem er sich hauptsächlich mit Experimenten zur Herstellung von Goldrubinglas und anderen Gläsern beschäftigte. Nach dem Tod des Großen Kurfürsten, der stets außerordentliches Interesse an den Arbeiten Kunckels zeigte, verlor dieser seine Stellung und wurde überdies der Veruntreuung bezichtigt. Das Laboratorium auf der Insel ging in der Folge durch Brandstiftung zugrunde. Kunckel wurde 1693 in Schweden als Bergrat angestellt und erhielt dort den Adelstitel »von Löwenstern«. Der Kaninchenwerder fiel an das Potsdamer Militärwaisenhaus.

Der Neffe und Nachfolger Friedrichs des Großen, Friedrich Wilhelm II., trachtete im Jahr 1793, den von ihm seit 1787 an den Ufern des Heiligen Sees bei Potsdam angelegten Landschaftsgarten, den Neuen Garten, zu erweitern. Nachdem der Bau eines gotischen Belvedere auf dem an der Rückseite des Neuen Gartens gelegenen Pfingstberg an den überhöhten Forderungen der Grundstückseigentümer gescheitert war, wandte der Monarch seine Aufmerksamkeit dem Kaninchenwerder, der heutigen Pfaueninsel, zu.[6] Vom 12. November 1793 datiert die Kabinettsorder Friedrich Wilhelms II. an seinen »lieben Cabinetsminister von Struensee«, die mit dem Satz beginnt: »Zu dem Amte Bornstedt gehört eine in der Havel liegende Insel, genannt der Kaninchenwerder, welche ich der Lage halber zu einigen Anlagen selbst übernehmen will.«[7] Von der anfangs geplanten unmittelbaren Vergrößerung des Neuen Gartens war es nun zu einer 4 km entfernten Erweiterung gekommen, die über die Havel hin in Sichtbeziehung zum Muttergarten steht. Doch mögen wohl noch andere Vorzüge des Eilands dem Monar-

Intimations on the Pfaueninsel
(dedicated to Martin Sperlich)

On a map, the Pfaueninsel, covering 166 acres[1], resembles a dolphin with a raised tail fin that has been forced to stop at the isthmus at Sacrow on its way to Potsdam. One can see very little of the island when one passes it in a boat, for the tall trees along its shores shield it almost completely from view. From the water, the theatrical white façades of the Castle and the Dairy are an enticing sight, but the Steward's House, Ferry House, Frigate Harbour and Hunting-Box are still waiting to be discovered behind their leafy screens. This mysterious, exotic atmosphere is heightened by the multifarious laments of the peacocks whose shrieks rise and fall like waves from the island's interior.

»It is above all our perceptions of our body's movements that provides us with an understanding of the garden as a spatial work of art«.[2] Martin Sperlich's succinct statement gives cogent expression to how we become familiar with a garden. This synthesis of the arts can obviously not be comprehensively or even thoroughly described, for not only must it be physically experienced, its many-sided nature is one of its artistic devices. For this reason, in my description of the Pfaueninsel, I have made conscious use of Fürst Pückler's highly appropriate term, »intimations«. The following pages can serve as no more than a sketch of the island's distinctive features, for if it is to be understood in its entirety, it must be visited.

The Pfaueninsel was developed as a synthesized work of art in two stylistic phases that reflected its special character. In the second phase the brilliant landscape architect, Peter Joseph Lenné used his considerable artistic powers to adapt what already existed and to render his vision of the garden in a form that was not only new but also much more complex and subtle. The first phase belongs to the era of the Romantic landscape garden and was initiated in 1793 by Gräfin Lichtenau – the confidante and erstwhile mistress of the Prussian monarch Friedrich Wilhelm II – by the monarch himself, and by the royal gardener Johann August Eyserbeck. From 1805 to 1816 the island was a »ferme orné«[3]. Today, almost no traces remain of this phase of development. Nevertheless, like the chrysalis that is necessary before the butterfly can emerge, these years were important as a transitional stage in the island's eventual transformation. During the second phase, from 1816 to 1834, the landscape garden was fully developed by Lenné in conjunction with Joachim Anton Ferdinand Fintelmann. Although far-reaching changes were made, the existing landscaping was not completely eradicated. Lenné took up the themes of the first phase but rendered them in diverse variations that were of a much greater artistic sensitivity. During this long creative process he did not work from a comprehensive design. Instead, his artistic imagination was repeatedly inspired by that which already existed, thereby refining and enhancing the island's appearance. Fürst Pückler has provided a superb description of this working method: a method that differs sharply from that used by architects.[4] In contrast to the preceding phase, this second phase saw the participation of the architect Karl Friedrich Schinkel whose abilities were at the very least equal to those of the landscape architect. Without the efforts of these two great artists, this landscape garden would have remained in its naive vernacular. They intensified and emebellished what already existed without destroying it. Taken by itself, no single architectural object on the island has either the aura or the significance that it has when it is seen as a part of the overall impression that the island makes. Lenné's garden is a composition of great complexity, where each building has been assigned its place, and it is ultimately the garden that holds everything together and endows it with meaning.

The island's charms were already appreciated a long time ago. Traces of settlements that reach back to the Bronze Age and the era of Slavic migrations have been found here. In the following centuries the island remained a romantic wilderness and was traversed primarily along its waterways. It was not until the reign of the Great Elector that it acquired a measure of historical significance, albeit still of a modest nature. In 1683, a rabbit hutch was installed at its western point, close to where the Castle stands today. Approximately

1. »Plan von der Gegend um Potsdam aufgenommen und entworfen durch C. G. von Tschirschky 1786«. Ausschnitt. (Staatsbibliothek zu Berlin – Preußischer Kulturbesitz, Kart. N 5931)

1. »Plan of the area around Potsdam, drawn and designed by C. G. von Tschirschky, 1786.« Detail. (Staatsbibliothek zu Berlin – Preußischer Kulturbesitz, Kart. N 5931)

chen den Wechsel vom Berg zur Insel attraktiv gemacht haben. Die Erinnerung an Kunckels Treiben auf der Insel war lebendig geblieben und wird ihr in den Augen des heftig zum Okkultismus neigenden Königs, der Mitglied des Rosenkreuzerordens war, eine magische Aura verliehen haben. Die Entdeckung der Südseeinseln und die dort in Natur und Gesellschaft vorgefundenen paradiesischen Verhältnisse, über die Louis-Antoine de Bougainville 1771[8] und als Begleiter der Cookschen Weltumsegelung Georg Forster 1777[9] begeistert berichteten, lösten in den Salons Europas eine regelrechte Insel-Passion aus, der freilich durch Rousseaus »Zurück zur Natur« der Boden bereitet war. Der König muß der Bewahrung des Wildnishaften auf der Insel großen Wert beigemessen haben, bestätigt doch der Minister einen Tag nach Erhalt der Kabinettsorder die Weitergabe des Befehls, daß auf dem »Caninchen Werder nicht das geringste an Holtz- oder Buschwerk weiter gefället werde«.[10] Die Gestaltung der Insel unter Friedrich Wilhelm II. macht diese Grundidee dann offenbar. Ihr Kern mit etwa 400 Uralt-Eichen blieb, sieht man von einer Scheune und einem Wegekreuz ab, unberührt, gleichsam Wildnis. Nur die dem Neuen Garten zugewandte Westspitze und das sumpfig-flache Nordostende der Insel wurden mit Bauwerken versehen. Zeitgenössische Erörterungen zur Gestaltungsidee der Insel finden sich nur in Form der schon nachträglichen Beschreibung von 1798, die einem Inventar aus demselben Jahr folgt.[11]

Bei den Bauten auf der Insel wurde recht ungewöhnlich verfahren. Weder das Potsdamer Hofbauamt noch das Berliner Oberhofbauamt wurden beteiligt; die Verantwortung trug allein der Potsdamer Zimmermeister Johann Gottlieb Brendel, der als Architekt, Bauleiter und Unternehmer fungierte. Die oberste Leitung der Pfaueninselbauten lag in den Händen des Geheimkämmerers Johann Friedrich Ritz. Auch traf der König selbst gelegentlich an Ort und Stelle seine Anordnungen. Die Mitwirkung des Oberhofbaudirektors Michael Philipp Boumann ist nur in zwei Fällen belegt. Stilistische Vergleiche legen die Vermutung nahe, daß für die Ausführung des boisierten Festsaals im Schloß Entwürfe von Carl Gotthart Langhans benutzt wurden.[12] Der früheren Mätresse und damaligen Vertrauten des Königs, die, als Tochter des Waldhornisten Elias Encke in Dessau geboren (der Schöpfer des Wörlitzer Parkes, Fürst Friedrich Franz, zählte zu ihren Taufpaten),[13] im vorletzten Lebensjahr des Königs zur Gräfin Lichtenau avancierte,[14] wurden sämtliche Bauplanungen der Insel durch Brendel oder Ritz, mit dem sie durch eine Scheinehe verbunden war, zur Genehmigung vorgelegt und häufig von ihr geändert. Man kann davon ausgehen, daß diese geschmackssichere Frau mit dilettantischer Unbekümmertheit weitgehend die Anregungen gab. Das erhellt eindrucksvoll, wie sehr die Bauten auf der Pfaueninsel in dieser Phase ein integraler Bestandteil des sentimentalen Gartens waren, ja ganz dem damals noch gängigen Gartendilettantismus, einem Dilettantismus im besten Sinn, unterworfen waren.

Was heute Schloß heißt, nannte man 1798 »römisches Landhaus«. Mit seinem Bau wurde im Frühjahr 1794 begonnen, und mit Ausnahme der Türme war das Gebäude im Herbst desselben Jahres einschließlich der Deckenmalereien fertiggestellt.[15] Über dem massiv gewölbten Keller wurde das zweigeschossige Haus in Fachwerk, mit Backsteinen ausgefacht, errichtet. Bekleidet wurde das Fachwerk mit Bohlen, deren Aussehen man durch Einwerfen von Quarzsand in die weiße Ölfarbe »versteinerte«. Mit Ausnahme der Türme wurde die Fassade durch aufgemalte Quader gegliedert (1974/75 in dieser ursprünglichen Form wiederhergestellt). Den südlichen der beiden Rundtürme nimmt die sich in eleganter Linienführung hinaufschraubende Wendeltreppe ein. Sie führt bis zur Höhe der die beiden Türme verbindenden Brücke. Die ursprünglich als Ausdruck ehrwürdigen Verfalls aus rohen Baumstämmen gezimmerte Brücke wurde, da tatsächlich so vergänglich wie ihr Aussehen, 1807 durch die filigrane gußeiserne in gotischen Formen ersetzt. Die Vollendung der Innenausstattung dauerte bis zum Herbst 1795 und wurde, nachdem Madame Ritz am 13. Mai ihre Italienreise angetreten hatte, vom König mit regem Interesse begleitet. Die Wahl des Bauplatzes erklärt

800 rabbits were bred here annually, and the island's erstwhile name of »Pfauenwerder« (»Peacock Holm«)[5] was gradually changed to »Kaninchenwerder« (»Rabbit Holm«). Enclosures for rabbits had already been used in ancient Rome, and this custom would be continued in the Italian Renaissance and Baroque gardens, where the animals often lived on small islands. The most well-known example of this is the island for rabbits in the Park of Valsanzibio. Perhaps it was this which prompted the Great Elector to use the relatively remote island for this purpose. Only two years later, however, in 1685, the rabbits had to leave the island again. The only reminder of their presence would be the name, which would continue to be used for over a century. The Great Elector gave the island to his chamberlain, the chemist and glass specialist Johann Kunckel, who installed a secret laboratory on it. His experiments here were primarily directed towards the production of golden and red crystal, as well as other types of glass. After the death of the Great Elector – who had always been extremely interested in Kunckel's work – the latter lost his position and was also accused of embezzlement. The laboratory was subsequently destroyed by arson. In 1693 Kunckel went to Sweden, where he advised the monarch on mining techniques and was made a baron with the title of »von Löwenstern«. The island was given to the home for soldier's orphans in Potsdam.

In 1793 Friedrich Wilhelm II, the nephew and successor of Frederick the Great, decided to expand the landscape garden, that he had begun to lay out in 1787 on the shores of the Heiliger See near Potsdam, the Neuer Garten. Initially, his plan was to build a Gothic belvedere on the Pfingstberg lying at the back of the Neuer Garten. Due to the excessive demands of the property owners, however, this plan came to nothing, and the monarch then turned his attention to Kaninchenwerder or as it is known today, Pfaueninsel.[6] On 12 November 1793 he sent an order of cabinet to his »dear cabinet minister von Struensee« that began with the statement: »In the district of Bornstedt there is an island lying in the Havel, known as Kaninchenwerder and because of its location I want to use it for park land«.[7] Instead of the original idea of a direct extension to the Neuer Garten, what was now foreseen was an extension that was clearly visible from this garden, even though it lay 4 km away, across the Havel. It is quite possible that this change from a mountain to an island had other attractions for the monarch. The nature of Kunckel's activities had not yet been forgotten, and this could well have bathed the island in a magical aura for the monarch, for he had strong leanings towards the occult and was a member of the Rosicrucian Order. The discovery of the South Sea Islands and their paradisal natural and social conditions had recently been described in glowing terms by Louis-Antoine de Bougainville in 1771[8] and by George Forster, who accompanied Cook on his circumnavigation of the globe in 1777[9]. At the time there was a veritable passion for islands in Europe's salons; a passion that had already been sparked by Rousseau's advocacy of a »return to a natural state«. The monarch clearly placed great importance on maintaining the island in its wild state, as can be seen in the response of the minister one day after he received the order of cabinet. He confirmed that the order would be passed on and that »not a single tree or bush will be cut down on Kaninchenwerder«.[10] This basic idea manifested itself in the work that Friedrich Wilhelm II undertook on the island. Apart from a barn and a wayside cross, its core of 400 ancient oaks was not touched, and it remained a wilderness. Buildings were only placed at its western point, facing the Neuer Garten, and on its flat, marshy north-eastern end. The only contemporary description of the design concept for the island dates from 1798, by which point these works had already been completed (earlier in this year an inventory had also been drawn up).[11]

The buildings on the island were rather unusual insofar as they were constructed without consulting the Hofbauamt in Potsdam and the Oberhofbauamt in Berlin. Instead a master carpenter from Potsdam, Johann Gottlieb Brendel, functioned as architect, building site manager and contractor, while the privy councillor Johann Friedrich Ritz was in overall charge of the project. Occasionally the monarch himself would come to the island and give orders on the work to be done. There are only two documented instances of the participation of the Oberhofbaudirektor Michael Philipp Boumann. Stylistic similarities allow for the assumption that designs by Carl Gotthart Langhans were used in the construction of the elaborately panelled banquethall in the Castle.[12] The monarch's confidante and for-

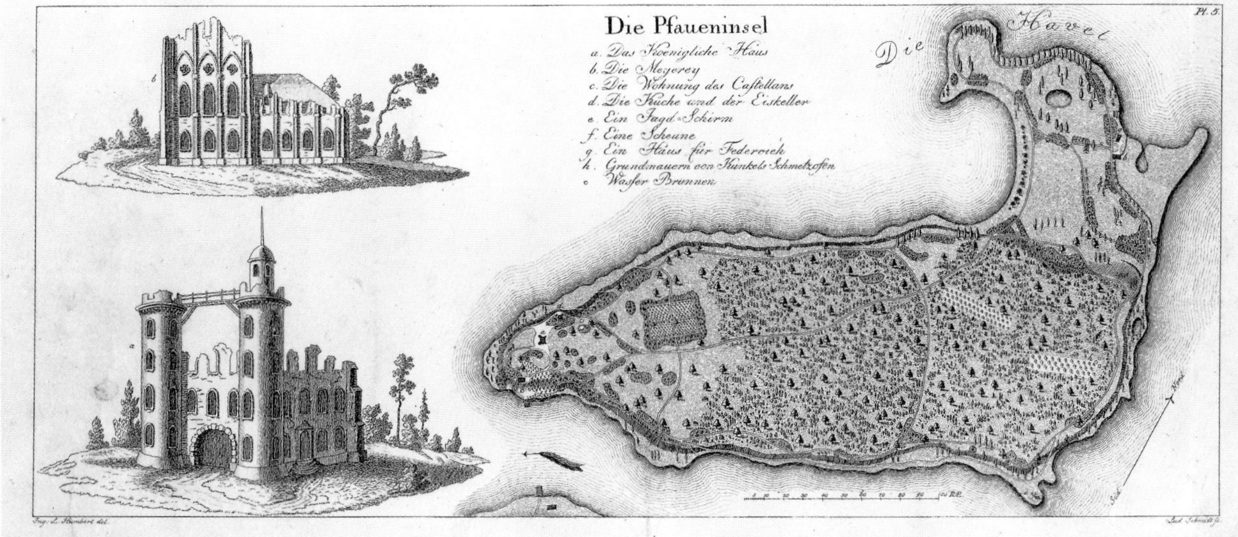

3. »Die Pfaueninsel«. Stich von Lud. Schmidt nach einer Zeichnung von L. Humbert, 1798.

3. »The Pfaueninsel«. Engraving by Lud. Schmidt after a drawing by L. Humbert, 1798.

sich aus dem Wunsch, das »römische Landhaus« als ferne Vedute von der Umgebung des Marmorpalais aus erleben zu können und der Insel von dieser Seite her ein unverwechselbares Attribut zu verleihen. Nur so ist die Ausrichtung der theaterhaften Schaufassade des Bauwerks und seine auf der Westspitze weit nach Norden geschobene Position zu erklären.

Die Anregung, ein zweitürmiges, durch eine Brücke verbundenes Gebäude auf dem Hohen Ufer der Insel zu errichten, scheint durch eine Ansicht der Insel Capri im 3. Band der *Voyage pittoresque ou description des Royaumes de Naples et Sicile* inspiriert zu sein.[16] Das von Abbé Richard de Saint-Non verfaßte fünfbändige Werk ist im Inventar der im Marmorpalais vor 1799 vorhandenen Bücher als Werk Nr. 1 verzeichnet.[17] Die Prachtbände sind vom König und der Gräfin Lichtenau bestimmt zur Vorbereitung der Italienreise benutzt worden. Saint-Non preist das angenehme Klima der Insel und schildert ihre bewegte Vergangenheit als Altersaufenthalt des Kaisers Augustus und als Ort der Ausschweifungen des Tiberius. So mag man in der Pfaueninsel zugleich mit Tahiti auch einen Abglanz des schönen Capri gesehen haben. Das bei Saint-Non auf der Tafel 98 abgebildete Bauwerk ist so klein und undeutlich, daß es nicht als Vorlage zum Bauen taugt, sondern nur einen Typus und seine landschaftliche Situation liefert. Beim Bauentwurf orientierte man sich an kompositionsähnlichen englischen Gartenstaffagen. Ungeklärt ist die Beziehung zu einem nicht realisierten Entwurf für einen Lustschiffhafen, den Michael Philipp Boumann für den Charlottenburger Schloßgarten gezeichnet hat. Die frappierende Ähnlichkeit dieses Bootshafens mit dem Schlößchen zwingt zu dem Schluß, Brendel habe sich den Entwurf zunutze gemacht und den Erfordernissen der Insel angepaßt. Oder hat Boumann die von Capri inspirierte Bauidee zweimal angeboten?

Während das Äußere des Schlosses durch die leeren Fensterhöhlen eines scheinbar untergegangenen dritten Geschosses Altehrwürdigkeit inszeniert und an die Vergänglichkeit allen Menschenwerks gemahnt, überrascht die Innenausstattung durch die hohe Kultur handwerklichen Könnens, die in der vollendeten künstlerischen Anwendung »vaterländischen« (also einheimischen) Holzes kulminiert. Daß zeitweilig 17 Tischler mit verschiedenen Aufträgen im Schloß arbeiteten, läßt sich nicht nur durch die vom Zimmermann Brendel ausgeübte Bauleitung, sondern auch mit einer besonderen Wertschätzung dieses naturnahen Werkstoffs erklären. Der Festsaal im ersten Obergeschoß, durch hölzerne Pilaster gegliedert und bis zum Gesims vertäfelt, ist in dieser Hinsicht ein besonderes Glanzstück. Weit öffnen sich seine sieben hohen Rundbogenfenster zur Seenlandschaft der Havel. Seine Decke ziert eine Kopie nach Guido Renis berühmter Aurora im Casino Rospigliosi, zu deren beiden Seiten Kopien des Apollo mit Hyacinth und Jupiter mit Ganymed nach Annibale Carraccis nicht weniger bekannten Fresken im Palazzo Farnese gesellt sind. Die häufig vermutete Beziehung zwischen den Rom-Elementen der Bauten der Pfaueninsel und der Reise der Gräfin Lichtenau nach Italien besteht nicht, wie sonst so häufig, in Reisereminiszenzen, sondern in der vorauseilenden sehnsuchtsvollen Beschäftigung mit Rom und Italien, denn als die »Bauherrin« Mitte Mai 1795 nach Italien aufbrach, waren die Bauten der Insel und deren Ausstattung weitgehend fertiggestellt. Madame Ritz hatte ihrem königlichen Freund etwas von einem vermeintlich römischen Ambiente auf der Insel hinterlassen, als sie die lang ersehnte Reise antrat, auf der er sie so gern begleitet hätte.

Zu den römischen Motiven zählt auch der ursprünglich im Zentrum einer regelmäßig angelegten Baumschule stehende Brunnen (seit Lenné nach 1816 die Baum-

4. »Das Königliche Schloss auf der Pfaueninsel«. Gouache von Wilhelm Barth, um 1805. (Staatliche Museen zu Berlin – Preußischer Kulturbesitz, Kupferstichkabinett)
5. Ansicht der Insel Capri von Osten. Stich von Longueil nach einer Zeichnung von Chatelet. (Jean-Claude Richard, abbé de Saint-Non, *Voyage pittoresque ou description des Royaumes de Naples et de Sicile,* Bd. 3, Paris 1783, Tafel 98)

4. »The Royal Castle on the Pfaueninsel«. Gouache by Wilhelm Barth, c. 1805. (Staatliche Museen zu Berlin – Preußischer Kulturbesitz, Kupferstichkabinett)
5. View of the Island of Capri from the east. Engraving by Longueil after a drawing by Chatelet. (Jean-Claude Richard, abbé de Saint-Non, *Voyage pittoresque ou description des Royaumes de Naples et de Sicile,* vol. 3, Paris 1783, plate 98)

mer mistress, Wilhelmine Encke, received all of the building plans for inspection and approval by Brendel or Ritz (a marriage undertaken as a pure formality linked her to Ritz). The daughter of a French horn player, she was born in Dessau and the creator of the Wörlitz park, Fürst Friedrich Franz was one of her godparents.[13] In 1797, one year before the monarch's death, she was given the title of Gräfin Lichtenau.[14] She often altered the plans that were presented to her and it is safe to assume that this woman of innate good taste continued to provide ideas with the care-free ease of the dilettante. This is a telling indication of how the buildings that were constructed on the Pfau-eninsel during this first phase were still an integral part of the dilettantism – in the best sense of the word – that prevailed at this time.

What is known as the Castle today, was called a »Ro-man Villa« in 1798. Construction on this building began in the spring of 1794 and, with the exception of the towers but including the ceiling paintings, was com-pleted by the autumn of the same year.[15] A two-sto-reyed half-timbered house with brick infill was placed on top of a solid, vaulted cellar. By adding quartz sand to the white oil paint, the thick boards cladding the framework were given the appearance of stone. With the exception of the two towers, the façade was paint-ed to make it look as if it were made of square stone blocks (restored 1974/75 to its original form). The southern rounded tower contains an elegant, twisting, spiral staircase. It leads to a bridge that lies on the same height as the towers that it connects. This bridge was originally constructed out of untreated wood and was thereby meant to lend expression to the dignity of the decay process. Because it really was as transitory as it looked, it was replaced in 1807 by a cast iron filigreed bridge in the Gothic style. Work was not completed on the Castle's interior until the autumn

of 1795. After Madame Ritz's departure for Italy on 13 April the monarch followed its progress with lively interest. The location of the building site meant that the »Roman Villa« could be seen from the area around the Marble Palace in Potsdam, and the small Castle provided this side of the island with a distinctive attrib-ute. This is the only explanation for the Castle's theatri-cal sham façade and for the fact that its position on the island's western point was pushed very far to the north.

The idea of placing a building with two bridged towers on the island's shore was probably inspired by a view of the island of Capri that appeared in the third volume of *Voyage pittoresque ou description des Royaumes de Naples et Sicile*.[16] In a catalogue (1799) of the books in the Marble Palace's library, this five-volume work by Abbé Richard de Saint-Non was listed in first place.[17] These sumptuous volumes would certainly have been used by the monarch and Gräfin Lichtenau in preparation for her Italian journey. Saint-Non praised Capri's pleasant climate and described its eventful past as the residence of the aged Emperor Augustus and the site of Tiberius' dissipations. It is possible, therefore, that not only Tahiti but also the beautiful is-land of Capri served as an example for the Pfauenin-sel. The building that is shown (Nr. 98) in Saint-Non's work is so small and indistinct that rather than being used as a model it probably provided ideas for a build-ing type and for the surrounding scenery. In composi-tional terms the design for the Castle was orientated towards the follies in English gardens. It is not clear, however, what role one should assign to Michael Phil-ipp Boumann's unexecuted design for a pleasure-boat harbour in the Charlottenburg Schloßgarten. There is an astonishing similarity between this design and the one for the Pfaueninsel Castle, and one can only conclude that Brendel used this design and

schule aufhob, begrenzt der Brunnen den Rand der »Großen Sicht«. Er wurde mit der »Maske« einer Ruinenarchitektur verkleidet, wie die zeitgenössische Beschreibung das Theaterhafte der Inselbauwerke charakterisiert. Die später als Jacobsbrunnen bekannte Architektur hatte damals weder Namen noch Erklärung und ist möglicherweise gerade deshalb ein verschlüsseltes Geheimnis, das sich nur dem Eingeweihten erschließt. Nicht unwichtig ist in diesem Zusammenhang, daß die Baumschule auf Anraten des Ministers Johann Christoph von Wöllner, der die führende Kraft der am Hof Friedrich Wilhelms II. einflußreichen Rosenkreuzer war, angelegt wurde. Über dem Brunnenschacht ist aus Sandstein die Ecke einer Tempelrückwand mit Giebel- und Gebälkfragment errichtet. Vorbild dazu sind die Reste der Cella des Serapistempels[18] am Westhang des Quirinal in Rom. Der Bildhauer Angermann und der Steinmetz Ludwig David Trippel haben offenbar als Vorlage für ihre Brunnenverkleidung einen seitenverkehrten Stich nach Etienne Du Pérac benutzt und den mittelalterlichen Treppenturm des Palazzo Colonna zu einem recht sinnlosen Pfeiler stilisiert. Als sie dieses verkleinerte Abbild schufen, war das Urbild als Ganzes bereits seit 180 Jahren zerstört und nur noch in umherliegenden Fragmenten erhalten. Ein geläufiges römisches Reisezitat kann damit also kaum aufgerufen worden sein, sondern eine Anspielung auf tiefere Zusammenhänge. Dieses Architekturfragment scheint auch kein zweites Mal zitiert worden zu sein. Recht unwahrscheinlich, aber möglich ist, daß in Kreisen der Rosenkreuzer dieses Bauwerk schon damals in Beziehung zum Serapiskult gebracht wurde. Der Name des aus Ägypten stammenden Gottes ist die gräzisierte Form von Osiris-Apis. Diese in ihrer Bedeutung schillernde Gottheit der Heilung und Rettung wurde zuerst in Alexandria, später im ganzen römischen Reich verehrt. Dies läge ganz auf der Linie des rosenkreuzerischen Interesses an orientalischen Kulten, das sich im Neuen Garten unter anderem mit der Aufstellung der Statue der Diana von Ephesos, zweier ägyptischer Gottheiten, einer Sphinx und einer Pyramide manifestierte. Auch wenn ein Serapis-Bezug entsprechend dem offiziellen Wissensstand nicht gegeben war, so war durch den vermeintlichen Tempel des Sonnengottes Sol gleichermaßen der orientalische Bezug hergestellt, da in der römischen Kaiserzeit mehrfach kleinasiatische Gottheiten im Sol-Kult vereint wurden. Der erst viel später auftauchende Name Jacobsbrunnen scheint eine Benennung nach einer nicht mehr bekannten Person zu sein.

Erst während der Ausbauarbeiten im »römischen Landhaus« muß der König den Entschluß gefaßt haben, darin die Pfaueninsel als einen Abglanz und Traum von Tahiti darzustellen. Das untere runde Turmzimmer wurde, obwohl hierfür bereits Boiserien angefertigt worden waren, mit grauer Leinwand ausgeschlagen und von Peter Ludwig Burnat und Peter Ludwig Lüdtke als »otaheitische Hütte« ausgemalt. Zwischen den realen Fenstern zeigen gemalte Ausblicke sowohl das Schloß auf der Pfaueninsel als auch das Marmorpalais unter tropischer Vegetation. Wie, um die Aussage Georg Forsters, der die Ähnlichkeit der Bewohner Tahitis mit den alten Griechen konstatierte,[19] sichtbar zu machen, wurde in die Kuppel der Bambushütte »eine milchweiße Glaslampe in Bronze nach griechischer Manier gefaßt« gehängt. Das ge-

samte Schlößchen enthält nur neun größere Räume. Das Erdgeschoß unterscheidet sich deutlich von der Beletage, die höher ist und in der die an den Festsaal anschließenden zwei Räume einschließlich der hochgewölbten Decken mit ostindischem Zitz bespannt sind, während die Wände des Erdgeschosses Papiertapeten zieren. Auffällig sind die zwischen den Fenstern angebrachten, mit Schnitzwerk gerahmten und bekrönten Spiegel. Im Obergeschoß reichen sie bis zum Boden und verschmelzen so die Räume virtuell mit dem umgebenden Park. Die Wände des dem Otaheitischen Kabinett im Erdgeschoß benachbarten Teezimmers zeigen 29 allegorische Gipsreliefs auf Gipsporphyr von Johann Peter Echtler. Wenn auch kein zusammenhängendes Programm abzulesen ist, so sind diese meist auf antiker Mythologie fußenden Allegorien doch zu Beziehungsgruppen zusammengefaßt. Sie bieten geistreicher Konversation Gelegenheit zu mannigfachen Anknüpfungen und Anspielungen. Besonders durch das benachbarte Otaheitische Kabinett drängen sich Parallelen zwischen dem goldenen Zeitalter der Antike und der neuentdeckten Glückseligkeit tropischer Inselwelten auf. In der Spannung zwischen diesen beiden Räumen werden wie an keiner anderen Stelle des Schlößchens die Träume und Ideale seiner Erbauer spürbar. Von außerordentlichem Reiz ist, daß die von der Gräfin Lichtenau bestimmte Innenarchitektur und Möblierung bis heute unverändert erhalten ist. Die Zeit Friedrich Wilhelms III. hat diesem Interieur nur einige Möbel, Bilder und biedermeierliche Erinnerungsstücke hinzugefügt.

Die im englischen Landschaftsgarten als Symbol für mittelalterliche Tugend und Freiheit stehende Gotik war in der Welt der Freimaurer und Rosenkreuzer auch sichtbare Verbindung zum Tempelherrenorden, in dessen Nachfolge man sich sah. So enstand auf der Insel 1½ km vom »römischen Landhaus« entfernt, jenseits des zauberhaft wilden Eichenwalds am Ostufer auf feuchtem Wiesenland eine Meierei, die »ein eingefallenes gotisches Gebäude vorstellt«. Der Bauplatz wurde so weit nach Norden hin gewählt, daß sich dem im Boot von Potsdam Nähernden, die weißen Doppeltürme des Schlosses vor Augen, links hinter der grünen Masse des Eichenwalds zugleich die Schaufassade der wie das Schloß weiß gestrichenen Meierei frei in flacher Wiesenlandschaft zeigt. Das ebenfalls von Brendel errichtete Bauwerk greift wiederum Motive englischer Gartenstaffagen auf. Das Vorbild der Ruine der »priory« in William Shenstones Landschaftsgarten The Leasowes ist unverkennbar.[20] Dem Streben des späten 18. Jahrhunderts nach der Tugendhaftigkeit und Gesundheit des Landlebens unter Berufung auf Vergil hatte sich eine neue Komponente hinzugesellt, die Apotheose der Milch. In Rambouillet war für Marie-Antoinette mit der Laiterie geradezu ein Tempel der Milch erbaut worden. Die Meierei auf der Pfaueninsel inszeniert die damals in der Mark Brandenburg häufig anzutreffende Situation, daß sich in den teilweise ruinösen Gebäuden einer säkularisierten Klosteranlage eine Domäne oder Bauernwirtschaft eingenistet hat. In dem Anbau eines Turmstumpfes, dessen Bekrönung mit ruinösen Fensteröffnungen verlorene Höhe andeutet, ist ein Kuhstall untergebracht. Neben der kleinen Meierwohnung im Untergeschoß des Turmes fanden die in der Milchwirtschaft dilettierenden Majestäten in einer Molkenstube die nötigen Utensilien, Butterfässer und Milchgefäße, in einem gotischen

adapted it to the island's requirements. On the other hand, it is possible that Boumann offered this Capri-inspired design on two separate occasions.

With the empty window openings that seem to belong to a destroyed third storey, the Castle's exterior has been quite consciously fashioned to elicit veneration for the transitory nature of all of man's works. It is quite a surprising contrast, therefore, to enter the Castle's interior and be confronted with highly accomplished examples of craftsmanship. Nowhere is this more apparent than in the artistic use of wood from the »fatherland« (indigenous wood). On occasions, there were 17 carpenters carrying out different tasks in the Castle. The explanation for this is not only to be found in the way that Brendel (himself a carpenter) organized this work, but also in the fact that a particularly high value was placed on this natural material. The pièce de resistance is the panelled banquet-hall on the first storey which is articulated by wooden pilasters. Its seven high, rounded windows offer an expansive view of the scenery around the Havel. Decorating its ceiling is a copy of Guido Reni's famous fresco of Aurora in the Casino Rospigliosi. It is flanked by copies of Annibale Carracci's equally famous frescoes of Apollo with Hyacinthe and Jupiter with Ganymede in the Palazzo Farnese. It has often been assumed that there was a connection between the Roman elements in the buildings on the Pfaueninsel and Gräfin Lichtenau's Italian journey. This connection was not based on reminiscences – as is so often the case – but rather on her eager anticipation of the upcoming journey to Rome and Italy. When she left for Italy in the middle of May 1795, the buildings on the island and their interiors were almost complete. Madame Ritz's royal friend would dearly have liked to accompany her on the long-planned journey. Instead, she left him on the Pfaueninsel with a little bit of what they both took for Roman ambience.

One of the Roman motifs on the island is the well which originally stood in the centre of an evenly laid-out tree-nursery (after 1816, Lenné did away with the tree-nursery, and the well was placed at the edge of the »Grand View«). A contemporary account of the theatrical nature of the island's buildings describes the well as clad in a »mask« of architectural ruins. Subsequently known as Jacobsbrunnen (Jacob's Well), at the time that it was installed there was neither a name nor an explanantion for the well. Perhaps its cryptic nature was only meant to be deciphered by the initiated. In this respect it is not insignificant that the tree-nursery was laid out on the advice of Johann Christoph von Wöllner, a very influential figure in Friedrich Wilhelm's court and a highly-placed Rosicrucian. A corner of a temple wall, with fragments of a pediment and entablature, was fashioned out of sandstone and placed around the well. The model for this were the remains of the cella of the Serapis Temple[18] on the western slope of the Quirinal in Rome. For their well ornamentation, the sculptor Angermann and the stonemason Ludwig David Trippel apparently worked from an engraving by Etienne Du Pérac on which the sides had been transposed. They also made use of the engraving's medieval tower on the Palazzo Colonna, stylizing it into a rather pointless pillar. When they created this miniature representation, the original temple had already been destroyed for 180 years, and all that remained were scattered fragments. It is highly

unlikely, therefore, that they were simply quoting this ruin, familiar to everyone who visited Rome. They were almost certainly making allusions to more complex relationships. Moreover, this architectural fragment does not appear to have been cited a second time. Although it is not very likely, it is not impossible that Rosicrucian circles had already connected the Roman temple to the cult of the god, Serapis. This was the Greek name for the Egyptian god Osiris-Apis. This enigmatic god of healing and succour was first worshipped in Alexandria and then throughout the Roman empire. A reference to this god would have been in keeping with the Rosicrucian interest in Middle Eastern cults. This had already manifested itself in the Neuer Garten which contained statues of Diana of Ephesus, two Egyptian divinities, a sphynx and a pyramid. One must not assume too much here, however, for at this time the Roman temple had not yet been officially linked to Serapis. It was believed to be a temple of the sun god, Sol. Nevertheless, here too there was a connection to the Middle East, for in the Roman Empire divinities from Asia Minor were often combined in the Sol cult. It was only much later that the well was known as the Jacobsbrunnen, and it seems to have been named after a now unknown person.

It was probably while the interior work was being done on the »Roman Villa« that the monarch had the idea of using it to depict the Pfaueninsel as a reflection and a dream of Tahiti. Although elaborately carved wooden panelling had already been prepared for the lower, round tower room, this room was now covered with grey canvas and painted by Peter Ludwig Burnat and Peter Ludwig Lüdtke to resemble an »Otaheite hut«. Views of the Pfaueninsel Castle and of the Marble Palace – both standing in the midst of tropical vegetation – were painted between the room's windows. Georg Forster had remarked on the similarity between the Tahitians and the ancient Greeks,[19] and as if to make this comparison visible, a Greek-style bronze lamp with milky white glass was hung in the cupola of the bamboo hut. The entire Castle has only nine larger rooms. The ground storey is quite different from the storey above it. Not only is this storey much higher, the walls and vaulted ceilings of the two rooms leading from the banquet hall have been covered with East Indian cotton, while on the ground storey the walls are decorated with wallpaper. The mirrors between the windows are an impressive sight. Framed and crowned by carved wood, on the upper storey they reach to the floor, thereby almost creating a fusion between the rooms and the surrounding park. In the tea room beside the Otaheite Cabinet on the ground storey, the walls have been decorated with 29 plaster reliefs on plaster porphyry executed by Johann Peter Echtler. Although there is no single, overriding concept here, most of these reliefs depict allegories from ancient mythology and can be assigned to different thematic groups, whose diverse associations and allusions were meant to provoke witty conversation. The proximity of the neighbouring Otaheite Cabinet was obviously meant to evoke parallels between the golden age of antiquity and the recently discovered blissful world of the tropical islands. Nowhere else in the Castle do the dreams and ideals of the monarch and Gräfin Lichtenau appear in such a palpable form as in the charged relationship between these two rooms. It was the Gräfin who decided upon the Castle's interior de-

Interieur bereitgestellt. Ersteigt der solcherart an die
Brüste der Urmutter Natur zurückgekehrte Besucher
die ohne erkennbares Ziel in den Turm hinaufführende
Treppe, so wird hinter einer Galerie, auf der der Haus-
herr sich zeigen sollte, eine gotische Tür sichtbar, die
sich überraschend zu einem lichtdurchfluteten Saal
öffnet. Dieser ist in phantasievoller Neugotik von einem
der ersten Theatermaler der Zeit, Bartolomeo Verona,
nach einem Entwurf des schon genannten Michael
Philipp Boumann dekoriert. Hier konnte auf eleganten
Ottomanen der von dieser unerwarteten Szenerie
überraschte Besucher süße Milch oder Tee zu sich
nehmen. Die mehr bühnenbildhafte architektonische Treppenführung erinnert in ihrer Wirkung, nicht in
ihrem Aussehen, an Horace Walpoles Treppenhaus in
Strawberry Hill bei London.[21]
Dem »römischen Landhaus« wurden bald zwei weitere
Bauten zugesellt. Am Landungssteg entstand auf den
Fundamenten eines zuvor durch das Waisenhaus ge-
nutzten Gebäudes das Wohnhaus des Kastellans, ein
bewußt dörflich konzipiertes Haus mit zurückgesetztem Obergeschoß aus Fachwerk und vielfarbigen
Findlingen für Plinthe, Stützpfeiler und Fensterfaschen.
Als besonderen Ausdruck ländlicher Erdverbundenheit
wurde es in den zum Schlößchen hinaufführenden
Hang hineingebaut, so daß das Obergeschoß auf der
rückwärtigen Seite mittels einer Brücke zu ebener
Erde mit dem Garten verbunden werden konnte. Von
der Höhe des anderen Ufers erwies sich das weiß
über dem ockerfarbenen Kastellanhaus thronende
Schloß als eine bühnenbildhafte Komposition des Themas Burg und Dorf. Durch den hohen Baumwuchs ist
dieses später noch durch das Fährhaus und das
Schweizerhaus bereicherte Bild heute nur noch im
Winter erlebbar. Auch die in holländischen Formen
nördlich des Schlößchens erbaute Küche wurde ge-

gen den Hang gesetzt. Sie ist ein eingeschossiger, mit
flachem Blechdach gedeckter Ziegelbau und bleibt
deshalb von der Höhe des Schlößchens her unsicht-
bar. Auf dem südöstlichen Landvorsprung der Insel errichtete man 1796 einen auf Wunsch des Königs in
Beelitz abgebrochenen Jagdschirm. Das Holzgebäude
von 5 mal 3 Achsen wird durch rustizierte Pilaster gegliedert, die wie der ganze Bau mit Eichenrinde bekleidet sind. Einer eigentlichen Nutzung ist diese bis heute
erhaltene Hütte auf der Insel nie zugeführt worden.
Ihre Bedeutung besteht in der für die damalige Zeit
charakteristischen Demonstration, daß alle Architektur
ihren Ursprung in der Natur hat.
Wesentlich für die landschaftliche Gestaltung war die
Erhaltung der etwa 300 altehrwürdigen, teilweise bereits ruinösen Eichen. Dies zeigt deutlich der erste
Gartenplan mit der individuellen Darstellung dieser
Bäume. Der Befehl Friedrich Wilhelms II. vom November 1786, also bald nach der Thronbesteigung, »daß
viel Platanen und roß Castanien angepflanzt werden«,[22] galt auch für die Pfaueninsel, auf der bis zum
heutigen Tag viele majestätische Platanen davon zeu-
gen. Außerdem ist für diese Zeit die Anpflanzung von
Lärchen, Weymouthskiefern, Fichten und Birken für
die Insel belegt.
Die Insel unterstand damals noch dem Hofgärtner des
Neuen Gartens, Morsch dem Älteren, der nach den
Angaben des aus Wörlitz stammenden Gärtners Johann August Eyserbeck arbeitete. Nach der Ansied-
lung von Pfauen, die man vom benachbarten Gut
Sacrow bezog, wurde dem Kaninchenwerder im Mai
1795 der Name »Pfaueninsel« verliehen. In einem Brief
von Eyserbeck an Ritz vom 23.4.1795 lesen wir noch
»Caninchen Werder«[23], am 16.5.1795 sprach Brendel
in einem Bauanschlag zum Kastellanhaus bereits von
der »Pfauen Insel«[24].

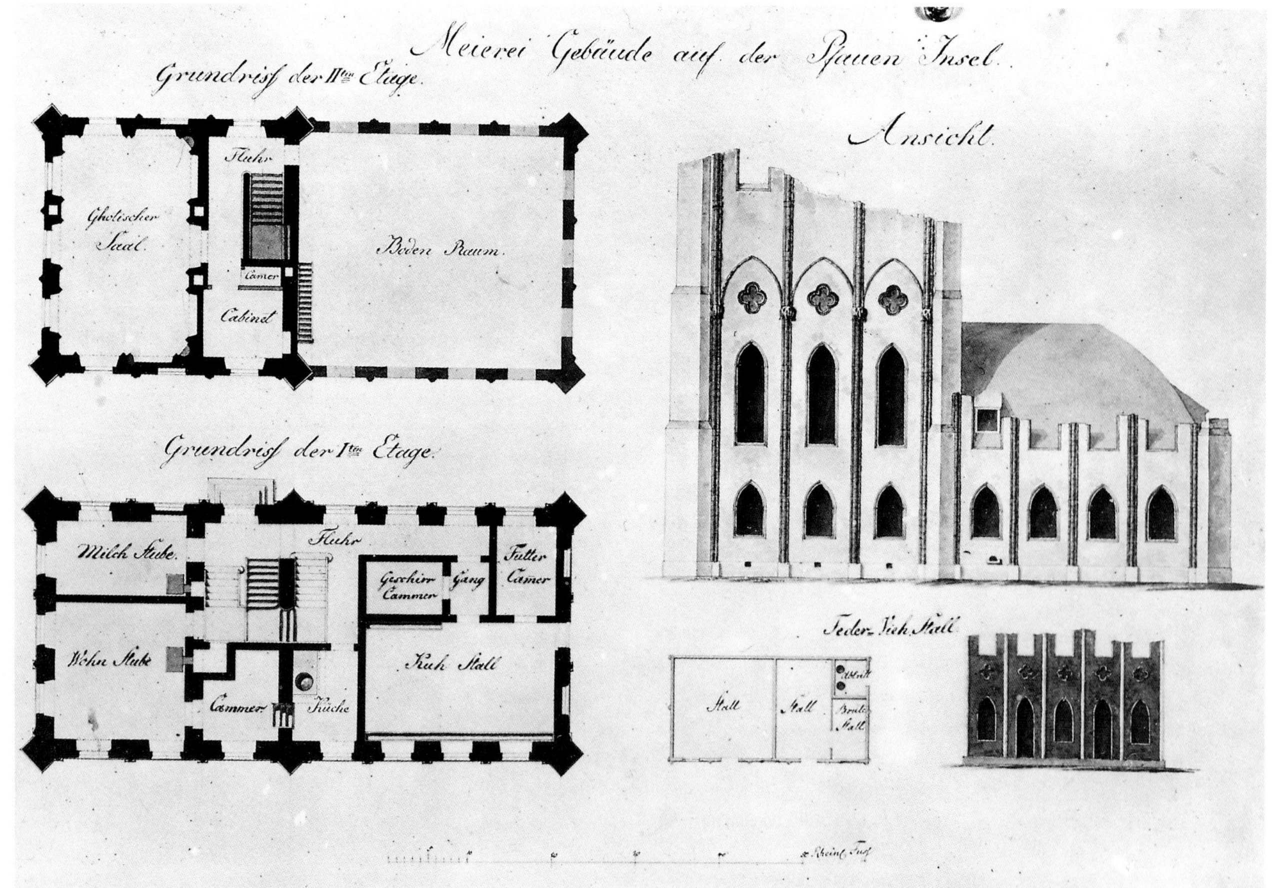

10. Die Meierei auf der Pfaueninsel. Bauaufnahme von
Carl Krüger, 1815. (Karl Brauer, *Die Pfaueninsel bei Berlin*, Berlin 1923, Tafel 9)

10. The Dairy on the Pfaueninsel. Drawing by Carl
Krüger, 1815. (Karl Breuer, Die Pfaueninsel bei Berlin,
Berlin 1923, plate 9)

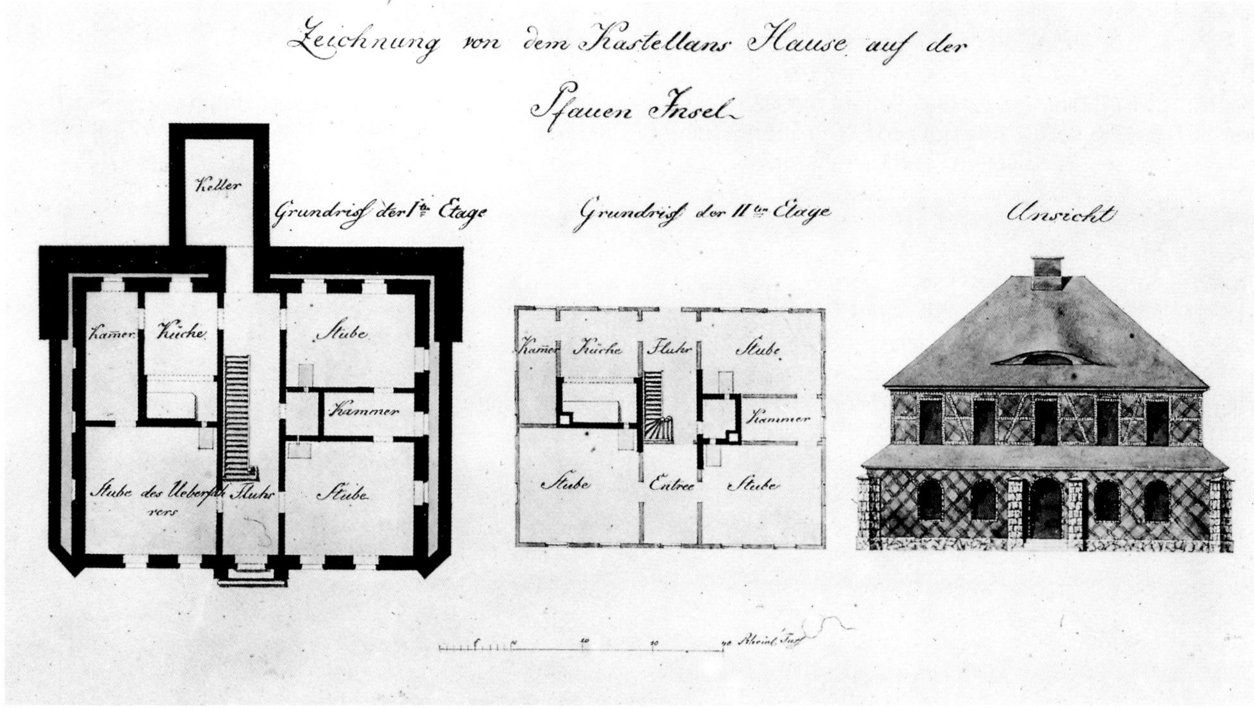

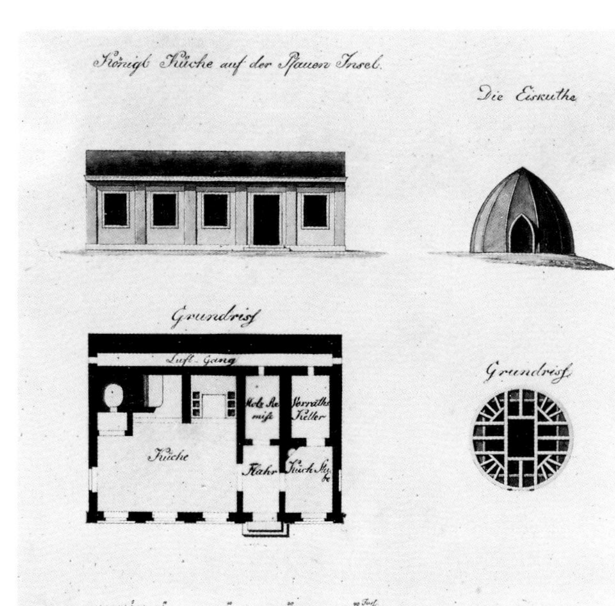

sign and furnishings, and the fact that these have remained unchanged to the present day is one of the Castle's special charms. During the reign of Friedrich Wilhelm III only a few pieces of furniture, pictures and Biedermeier keepsakes were added.

The Gothic Revival style evident in the English landscape gardens of the 18th century was meant to symbolize medieval virtues and freedom. This took on a particular significance for this century's Freemasons and Rosicrucians, for they understood themselves as the successors to the famous medieval order of the Knights Templar. On the island's eastern shore, 1½ km away from the »Roman Villa« and on the other side of an enchanting wild oak forest, a dairy, meant to »represent a medieval building fallen to ruin«, was built on a damp meadow. The reason for selecting a building site that lay this far north was to ensure the creation of a specific effect. When approaching the island from Potsdam in a boat, the Castle's two white towers are directly in one's line of vision, and if one looks to the left, behind the green mass of the wild oak forest, one equally sees the Dairy – its main façade also painted white – standing freely in the flat meadow. This building, also constructed by Brendel, takes up motifs of the English garden folly. There are unmistakable similarities with the ruin of the »priory« in William Shenstone's landscape garden The Leasowes.[20] The late 18th century's preoccupation with the virtuous and healthy nature of pastoral life, as it had once been described by Virgil, had now acquired a new component: the apotheosis of milk. In Rambouillet the dairy built for Marie-Antoinette was virtually a temple for milk. The dairy on the Pfaueninsel was not unusual for the Mark Brandenburg at this time, where similar installations, manors and farmyards, could be found in buildings (sometimes fallen to ruin) which belonged to secularied monasteries. Although the ruined window openings in the Dairy's tower stump were meant to indicate the building's former height, what the tower actually contained was a cow-shed. Beside a small dwelling on the tower's ground storey was a room with a Gothic interior where their majesties were able to

play »dairy«. The necessary utensils – butter kegs and milk jugs – were kept waiting for them. If the visitor, who has here returned to the primal bosom of Mother Nature, climbs the tower stairs – which do not seem to lead anywhere – he will encounter a Gothic door. Behind it lies a surprise: a large room, flooded with light. The room was decorated in an imaginative Neo-Gothic style by Bartolomeo Verona, one of the era's pre-eminent painters of stage sets. He worked according to a design by the afore-mentioned Georg Friedrich Boumann. Taken aback by this unexpected scenery, the visitor could recline on elegant ottomans and sip sweet tea or milk. The stairs have more to do with a stage set than with architecture. If not in their appearance, in their effect they recall Horace Walpole's stairwell at Strawberry Hill near London.[21]

Two further buildings were soon added to the »Roman Villa«. A house for the steward was built at the landing-stage on top of the foundations of a building that had been used by the orphanage. It was deliberately conceived as a house in a rural village, with a retracted, half-timbered upper storey and multi-coloured field stones for plinths, supporting pillars and window trimmings. To emphasize its connection to the land it was built into the slope leading up to the Castle, so that the back of the upper storey could be connected by a bridge to the garden. From the other shore one saw the white Castle enthroned over the ochre-coloured Steward's House: a theatrical composition on the subject of castle and village. This composition was later augmented by the Ferry House and the Swiss House, but because of the very high trees it is today only visible during the winter months. The Dutch-style kitchen building, constructed north of the Castle, was also placed against the slope. This one-storeyed brick building, with a flat metal roof, cannot be seen from the Castle. In 1796 a hunting-box, dismantled at Beelitz at the king's request, was erected on the island's south-eastern tip. The wooden structure with 5 x 3 axes is articulated by rusticated pilasters which, like the entire building, are clad in oak bark. The box, preserved to this day, was never actually put to any use.

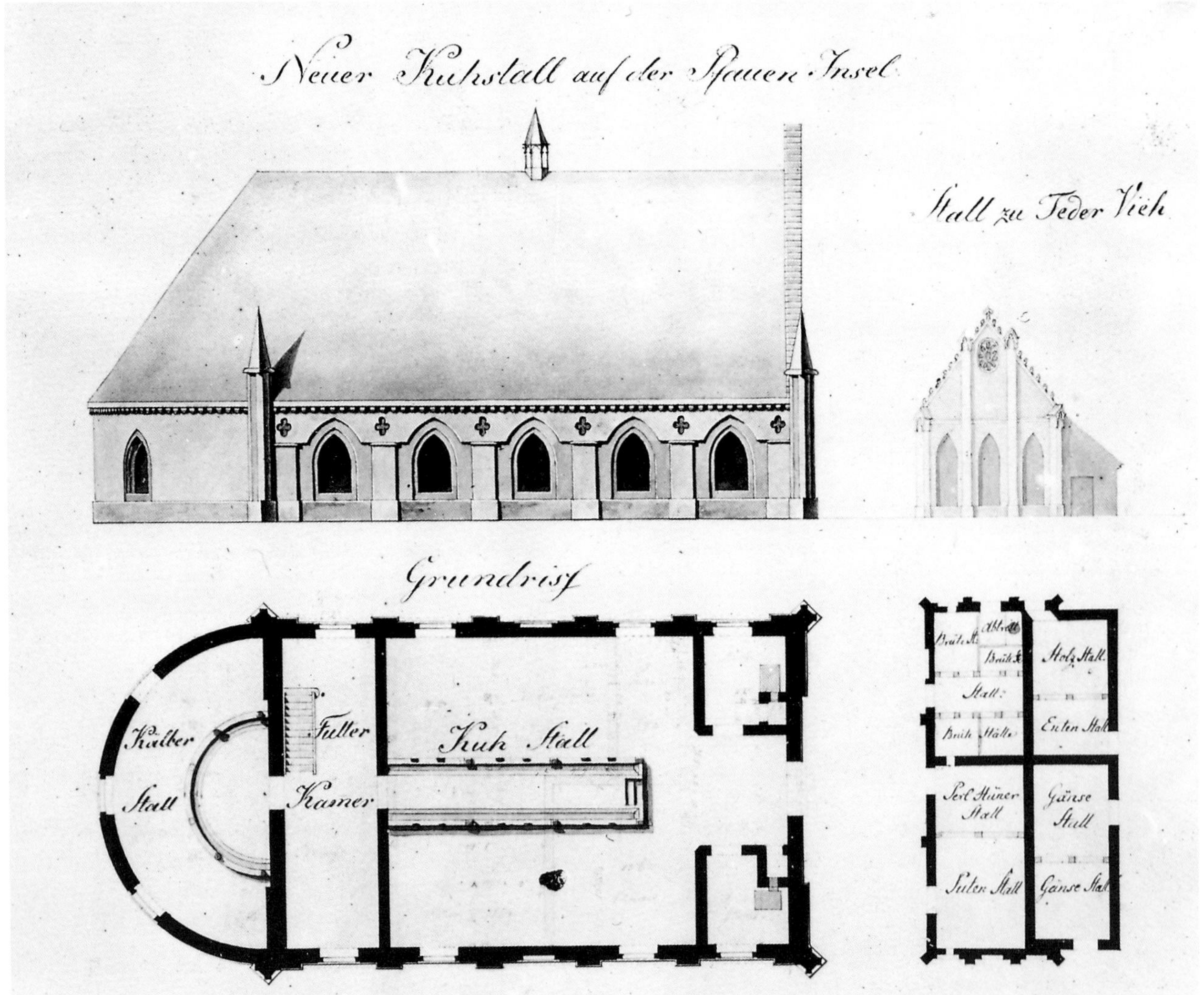

13. Die Meierei auf der Pfaueninsel. Aquarellierte Federzeichnung von Friedrich Wilhelm Delkeskamp, um 1820. (Stiftung Schlösser und Gärten Potsdam-Sanssouci, Aquarellslg. 483 a)

14. Der Kuh- und der Geflügelstall auf der Pfaueninsel. Bauaufnahme von Carl Krüger, 1815. (Karl Breuer, *Die Pfaueninsel bei Berlin*, Berlin 1923, Tafel 13)

13. The Dairy on the Pfaueninsel. Pen-and-wash drawing by Friedrich Wilhelm Delkeskamp, c. 1820. (Stiftung Schlösser und Gärten Potsdam-Sanssouci, Aquarellslg. 483 a)

14. The Cow-Shed and the Chicken-Coop on the Pfaueninsel. Drawing by Carl Krüger, 1815. (Karl Breuer, Die Pfaueninsel bei Berlin, Berlin 1923, plate 13)

Its significance lies in the fact that it provides a demonstration of the belief, characteristic of the time, that all architecture has its origins in nature.

The preservation of approximately 300 ancient oak trees – some of them already seriously damaged – was of fundamental importance in the island's landscape design. This is apparent in the first garden plan, in which these trees are individually depicted. Soon after his accession to the throne in November 1786 Friedrich Wilhelm II ordered that »many plane and chestnut trees« should be planted.[22] This order also applied to the Pfaueninsel and to the present day it boasts many majestic plane trees. At this time the island was also planted with larches, Weymouth pines, fir trees and birches.

The royal gardener Morsch the Elder, responsible for the Neuer Garten, was also in charge of the landscaping on the island. He worked according to the instructions of the gardener Johann August Eyserbeck who came from Wörlitz. After peacocks were introduced onto the island from the neighbouring estate of Sacrow, the name »Kaninchenwerder« was changed to Pfaueninsel in May 1795. In a letter to Ritz, dated 23 April 1795 Eyserbeck still referred to »Kaninchenwerder«[23] but in a cost estimate for the Steward's House, dated less than a month later (16 May 1795), Brendel referred to the Pfaueninsel.[24]

It is possible that a symbolic gesture was intended with the introduction of the peacock to the island. Its symbolic meanings are as iridescent as its plumage. In the Bible the peacock is a part of Solomon's glory. Peacocks were attributes of the Greek goddess Hera and the Roman goddess Juno and pulled their chariots through the heavens. Peacocks had been kept in the Heraion on the island of Samos since pre-Hellenic times.[25] The peacock's fanned tail was a symbol of the firmaments. The innumerable patterns or »eyes« on its wings represented the stars. Peacocks were important decorative elements in Roman gardens and were then used by the early Christians as symbols of

paradise and resurrection. There are endless connections that could be drawn here to the creators of the Pfaueninsel. Rather than selecting one interpretation, however, it seems most appropriate to allow for a variety of possibilities.

After the death of Friedrich Wilhelm II in 1797, his son Friedrich Wilhelm III – who had otherwise loathed everything to do with his father – quickly became the island's new admirer. Whereas his father had no longer had the chance to live on the island, Friedrich Wilhelm III and his young wife, Queen Luise, enjoyed the secluded rural life that they found here. (They had already developed a taste for this on their estate at Paretz, which the crown prince had acquired in 1795.) The young queen did complain in a letter, however, about the Castle's rather flimsy construction, »where neither lock nor bolt can guard one's privacy, for everything can be heard and thereby spoiled and betrayed. The walls are known to be made of paper and they betray your neighbour's every sigh«.[26] The ideal that Paretz represented was now taken up for the island and it was transformed into a farm, albeit one characterized by aesthetic considerations – a ferme ornée. This process was carried out by Joachim Anton Ferdinand Fintelmann, the royal gardener on the Pfaueninsel after 1804. In 1801 a shed for cows was added to the Dairy. Stylistically adapted to the original building, it resembled a Gothic chapel. In 1803/04 a double-towered guest house with the same rustic ornamentation as the Steward's House was built close to a barn in the centre of the island. On Fintelmann's tillage plan of 1806 there are no fallow periods foreseen for the six fields that have been cut out of the forest. They are to be tilled by rotating the crops. Here was a royal example of Thaer's agricultural reforms.[27] These fields were interspersed with the familiar veteran oak trees, all of which were preserved. In this dovetailing of park and agricultural terrain the island resembled Wörlitz. This extensive exposure of the ground's

15. Der Jagdschirm auf der Pfaueninsel. Ölgemälde, um 1802. (Ehemals Hohenzollernmuseum; Verwaltung der Staatlichen Schlösser und Gärten Berlin, Fotoarchiv)
16. Plan der Pfaueninsel mit Angabe der Feldbestellung. Aquarellierte Federzeichnung von Joachim Anton Ferdinand Fintelmann, 1810. (Verwaltung der Schlösser und Gärten Berlin, Schloß Pfaueninsel)

15. The Hunting-Box on the Pfaueninsel. Oil painting, c. 1802. (Formerly Hohenzollernmuseum; Verwaltung der Schlösser und Gärten Berlin, Fotoarchiv)
16. Plan of the Pfaueninsel showing tillage of fields. Pen-and-wash drawing by Joachim Anton Ferdinand Fintelmann, 1810. (Verwaltung der Schlösser und Gärten Berlin, Schloß Pfaueninsel)

Schillernd wie sein Gefieder ist die symbolische Bedeutung des Pfaus, an die man gedacht haben könnte, als man ihn auf die Insel brachte. Die Bibel kennt ihn als einen Teil der Herrlichkeit Salomos. Als Attribute der griechischen Hera und der römischen Juno zogen Pfauen den Wagen der Göttinnen durch das Himmelsgewölbe. Seit vorgriechischer Zeit wurden im Heraion auf der Insel Samos Pfauen gehalten.[25] Sein Rad war Gleichnis des Himmelsgewölbes, und die Augen seiner Federn standen für die Sterne des Firmaments. Der Pfau war wichtige Zierde reicher römischer Gärten und wurde dann für die frühen Christen Symbol des Paradieses und der Auferstehung. Unendlich ließen sich da Beziehungsfäden zu den Schöpfern der Pfaueninsel knüpfen. Dem Gegenstand am angemessensten scheint mir jedoch, die Vielfalt des Möglichen in der Schwebe zu lassen.

Nach dem Tod von Friedrich Wilhelm II. im Jahr 1797 erhielt die Insel in dessen Sohn und Nachfolger Friedrich Wilhelm III., der sonst dem väterlichen Wesen gänzlich abgeneigt war, schon bald einen neuen Liebhaber. Während dem verabscheuten Vater keine Zeit geblieben war, die Insel zu bewohnen, fand der Sohn hier mit seiner jungen Gemahlin, der Königin Luise, die ländliche Zurückgezogenheit, die das Kronprinzenpaar an dem Gut Paretz, das ihm seit 1795 gehörte, so schätzte. Die junge Königin klagte allerdings in einem Brief über den leichten Bau des Schlößchens, »wo kein Schloß und kein Riegel vor Einbruch bewahrt, da das Gehör alles verdirbt und verrät, was die klügste Vorkehrung gut machte, da bekanntlich die Mauern von Papier sind und jeden Seufzer verräterisch seinen Nachbar hören läßt«.[26] Die Insel erfuhr nun ganz folgerichtig nach Paretzer Ideal ihre Umwandlung in eine ästhetisch geprägte Landwirtschaft, eine »ferme ornée«. Diese Umgestaltung vollzog Joachim Anton Ferdinand Fintelmann, der seit 1804 Hofgärtner auf der nun eigenständigen Pfaueninsel war. 1801 wurde der Meierei in stilistischer Anpassung an den Ursprungsbau ein Kuhstall in Form einer gotischen Kapelle hinzugefügt und 1803/04 im Zentrum der Insel in der Nachbarschaft einer schon bestehenden Scheune ein zweitürmiges Kavalierhaus mit dem gleichen rustikalen Findlingsdekor wie das Kastellanhaus erbaut. Fintelmanns Feldbestellungsplan von 1810 zeigt sechs nach landschaftsgärtnerischen Vorstellungen aus dem bisherigen Waldgelände herausgehauene Felder, die, ohne Brache in Fruchtwechselwirtschaft bestellt, ein königliches Muster der Thaerschen Landwirtschaftsreformen darstellen.[27] Durchsetzt sind diese Felder mit den wohlbekannten Eichenveteranen, die sämtlich erhalten blieben. Mit dieser Anlage nähert sich die Insel dem Vorbild Wörlitz in seiner engen Verzahnung von Park und landwirtschaftlicher Nutzfläche. Die großflächige Freilegung der natürlichen Bodenmodellierung war eine wichtige Vorbereitung für die endgültige Gestaltung der Insel durch Peter Joseph Lenné, der »wie selten einer verstand, die Bodenformation zu individualisieren«.[28]

1816 erhielt der Hofgärtner Fintelmann den Auftrag, unter Hinzuziehung des erst in jenem Jahr vom Rhein nach Potsdam berufenen »Garteningenieurs« Lenné die Insel als Landschaftspark zu gestalten. Der als Reformer herbeigeholte Lenné wurde in den Potsdamer Hofgärtnerkreisen durchaus nicht mit Begeisterung

und Wohlwollen aufgenommen. Fintelmann, der Hofgärtner der Pfaueninsel, selbst ein fähiger Landschaftsgärtner, begegnete dem Neuling dagegen mit großer Sympathie, die zu einer lebenslangen, innigen Freundschaft wurde. Dies war für die nun folgende einzigartige Gestaltung der Insel von grundlegender Bedeutung. Lenné entwickelte dem verständnisvollen Freund seine Vorstellungen unmittelbar vor Ort. Daraus ergab sich ein fruchtbarer Dialog, der Fintelmann die Möglichkeit bot, auch eigene Ideen einzubringen. Die im Gelände vollendete Gestaltung wurde erst nachträglich in einem Plan festgehalten, der nicht von Lenné, sondern von Fintelmann gezeichnet wurde. Lennésche Entwurfspläne für die Pfaueninsel waren nicht nötig.

1819 erhielt die Insel, auf der es neben Schaukeln und Wippen bereits eine Kegelbahn gab, mit einem hölzernen russischen Rollberg ein Bauwerk, das nicht nur dem Vergnügen der königlichen Kinder und Enkelkinder diente, sondern auch allerhöchste Herrschaften erfreute. Der Monarch hatte ein Jahr zuvor anläßlich des Besuches bei seiner mit dem Zarewitsch vermählten Tochter eine derartige »Montagne russe« kennengelernt und für die Pfaueninsel ein Modell in Petersburg bestellt.[29] Eine vergleichbare Anlage läßt sich bereits 1665 unter Louis XIV. in Versailles nachweisen und wurde 1691 auch im Garten von Marly aufgestellt.[30] Zurückgehend auf berühmte russische Vorbilder, wie die Katalnaja Gorka im Park von Oranienbaum bei Petersburg, hatten die »montagnes russes« noch vor dem Bau der Anlage auf der Pfaueninsel in die Pariser Vergnügungsparks mit großem Erfolg Einzug gehalten.[31] Die heute nur noch als Fragment erhaltene Rutschbahn auf der Pfaueninsel war so geschickt in das Gehölz zwischen zwei Wege gesetzt, daß sie fast unbemerkt blieb. Sie zeigte sich auf beiden Seiten erst dann als interessante Überraschung, wenn man unmittelbar vor ihr stand.

Die Anlage des berühmten Rosengartens im Jahr 1821 steht am Anfang der tiefgreifenden Umgestaltung der Insel, die im Jahr 1834 ihren Abschluß fand. Als Ort für diesen ersten preußischen Rosengarten wählte Lenné die Südseite der großen Schloßwiese. Hier wurde in den sanften Höhenrücken ein flaches Tal gemuldet und mit dem so gewonnenen Boden die nach Norden abfallende Schloßwiese gefälliger modelliert. Den Rosengarten selbst legte Lenné in einer von ihm später niemals wiederholten landschaftlichen Form an. Im Ausgleich zwischen der Dynamik des umgebenden landschaftlichen Raumes und dem selbstvergessenen Tändeln dieses Rosengartens liegt das Ungewöhnliche seiner Plazierung und Gestaltung.

Aus der Vorliebe Friedrich Wilhelms III. für exotische Tiere hatte sich zwischen Kastellanhaus und Schloß eine kleine Menagerie mit Affen- und Adlerkäfig nebst einigen anderen Tierbehausungen entwickelt. Diesem auf Dauer unhaltbaren Zustand sollte Lenné durch die Neueinrichtung einer Menagerie im Zentrum der Insel abhelfen. Der König wollte die fremden Tiere nach dem Vorbild des Jardin des Plantes, den er 1815 in Paris kennengelernt hatte, auf der Insel verteilt wissen. Obwohl Lenné vom Jardin des Plantes hinsichtlich der Gestaltung der Gebäude und Gehege vielerlei Anregungen verarbeitete, ging er mit der breiten, von jeder einengenden Bebauung freigehaltenen Sichtachse, an deren Rändern er die Tiergehege gruppierte, einen eigenen, ganz neuen Weg. Seit 1824 wurden ein Adler-

natural forms would prove to be an important preparation for Peter Joseph Lenné's final reshaping of the island. He had »a rare understanding of how the ground's forms could be individualized«.[28]

In 1816 the royal gardener Fintelmann was instructed to work in conjunction with the »garden engineer« Lenné in shaping the island into a scenic park. (The latter had just been summoned from the Rhineland to Potsdam.) Lenné was known to be a reformer and encountered neither enthusiasm nor goodwill from most of the royal gardeners. In contrast, Fintelmann, the royal gardener responsible for the Pfaueninsel, who was himself a capable scenic gardener greeted the newcomer with a sympathy that would turn into a deep and lifelong friendship. This would be of fundamental importance in the subsequent unique reshaping of the island, where Lenné would present his ideas »on site« to his understanding friend. The ensuing fruitful dialogue also gave Fintelmann the chance to introduce some of his own ideas. A plan was only drawn up – by Fintelmann – once all of the landscaping had been completed. It was not necessary for Lenné to provide a design for the Pfaueninsel.
In 1819 a wooden slide – a »montagne russe« – was added to the island's swings, seesaws and skittle alley and was greatly enjoyed by the monarch's children and grandchildren as well as by more exalted personages. In the preceding year, while visiting his daughter who was married to the tsarevich, the monarch had ordered a »montagne russe« for the Pfaueninsel in Petersburg.[29] As early as 1665 Louis XIV had already had a slide installed at Versailles, and one was also installed in the Marly gardens in 1691.[30] Before the construction of the slide on the Pfaueninsel »montagnes russes«, such as the Katalnaja Gorka in the Oranien-baum Park near Petersburg, were the models for similar and hugely popular constructions in Parisian amusement parks.[31] Today, only a fragment remains of the slide that was built for the Pfaueninsel. It was placed so skilfully between two paths in the copse that it went almost unnoticed. This interesting surprise only became visible when one stood directly in front of it and saw both of its sides.

The famous Rose Garden was laid out in 1821. This marked the beginning of a series of far-reaching changes on the island which would be completed by 1834. The site chosen by Lenné for Prussia's first rose garden was the southern side of the large meadow surrounding the Castle. Although the meadow dropped off to the north, this was rectified with the soil gained from the flat depression hollowed out of its ridges. Lenné laid out the Rose Garden in a landscaped form that he would never use again. Its location and layout are unusual in the way that they effect a balance between the dynamics of its detached, dal-lying nature and the surrounding scenery.

Friedrich Wilhelm III had a predilection for exotic animals. Over time a small menagerie that included apes and eagles was kept in cages located between the Steward's House and the Castle. This situation could not be allowed to continue indefinitely and Lenné was instructed to provide facilities for a menagerie at the centre of the island. The monarch wanted the animals to be distributed in a manner similar to that of the Jardin des Plantes, which he had seen in Paris in 1815. In his fashioning of the buildings and compounds Lenné was certainly often stimulated by the Jardin des Plantes. At the same time, however, he also followed an entirely individual and completely new path by creating a visual axis that was free of all constricting buildings. The animal compounds were grouped at the

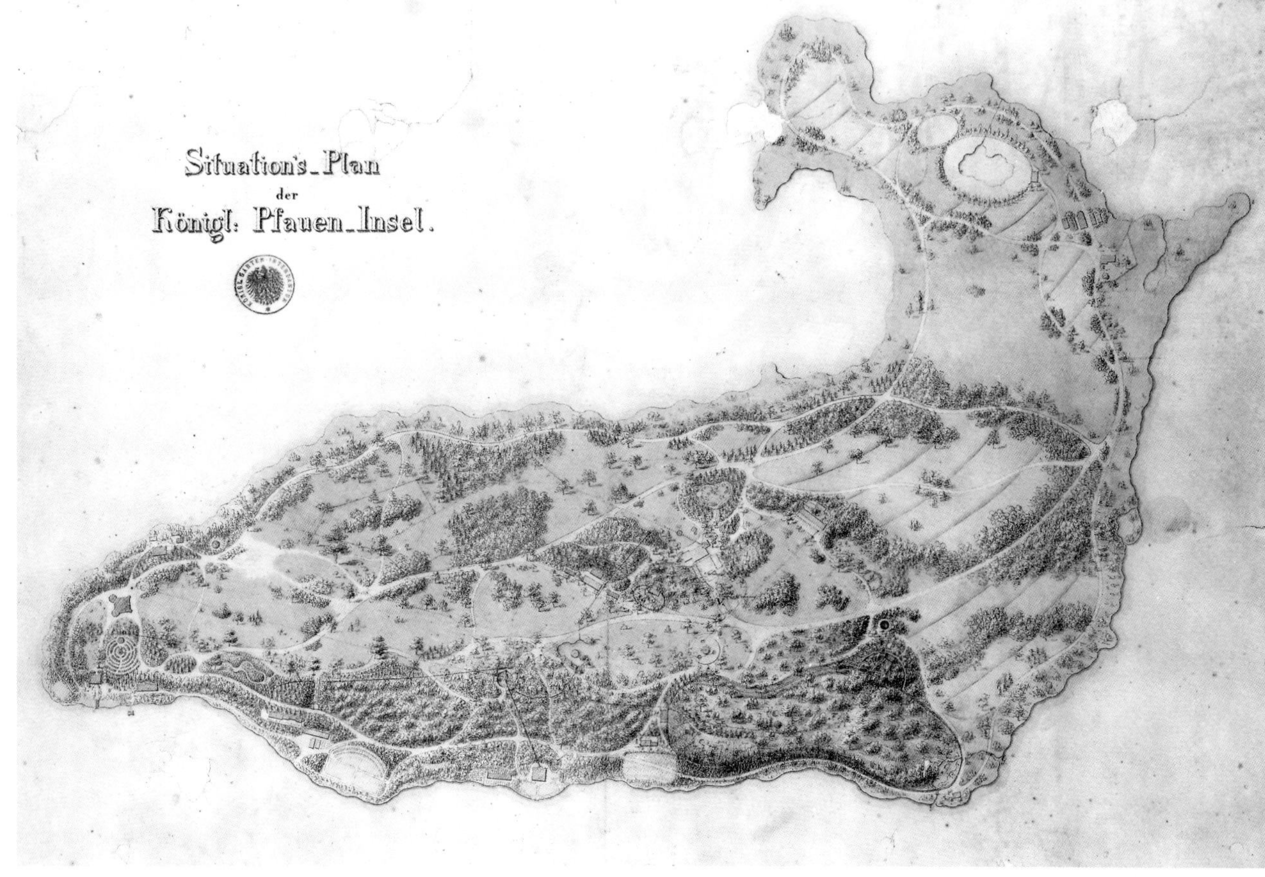

18. »Situation's-Plan der Königl: Pfauen-Insel«. Aquarellierte Federzeichnung von Joachim Anton Ferdinand Fintelmann, 1828. (Verwaltung der Staatlichen Schlösser und Gärten Berlin, Pk 1906)

18. »Topographical plan of the Royal Pfaueninsel«. Pen-and-wash drawing by Joachim Anton Ferdinand Fintelmann, 1828. (Verwaltung der Staatlichen Schlösser und Gärten Berlin, Pk 1906)

käfig, ein Affenhaus, eine Voliere und ein in einem künstlichen Teich stehendes Haus für fremde Wasservögel erbaut und die gotische Fasanerie aus dem Neuen Garten zur Insel gebracht und vergrößert.

Um 1824 wurde zwischen dem Kastellanhaus und dem Schloß im Bereich der abgebrochenen Tierkäfige ein in sich abgeschlossener kreisrunder Blumengarten aus konzentrisch angeordneten Wegen und Beeten angelegt. In diesem, Runder Garten genannten, von der Umgebung durch Pflanzungen ausgesonderten Bezirk reihen sich wie auf den Rängen eines Theaters die schönsten Blumen jeder Jahreszeit. Eine am Rand angebrachte Laube ermöglicht es, sich in die Betrachtung dieser nur hin und wieder durch einen Pfau gestörten Blumenkreise zu versenken.

Gleichzeitig mit der Errichtung der Menageriebauten erhielt die Insel eine künstliche Gartenbewässerung, die erste, die in einem brandenburgischen Garten dauerhaft funktionierte. In dem eigens dafür am Südufer der Insel erbauten soliden Wohnhaus des talentvollen Maschinenmeisters förderte eine englische Dampfmaschine das Flußwasser in ein rundes Reservoir auf dem höchsten Punkt der Insel. Man wußte das technisch Notwendige künstlerisch zu überhöhen, indem man in das Becken einen gußeisernen römischen Schalenbrunnen stellte, über den sich die gesamte Wassermenge in das Becken ergießt. Dies geschah zum ersten Mal am 3. August 1825 im Beisein und am Geburtstag des Königs. Den Schalenbrunnen bezeichneten die Zeitgenossen mit dem seit alters her in Anspielung auf die antiken Kerzenhalter gebräuchlichen Namen »Candelabre«. Zugleich wird damit ein geistvoller Bezug zu der lichtgleichen Wirkung des Wassers

hergestellt. Der Umstand, daß das Fontänenrund bei seiner Anlage von hohen, knorrigen Eichen umstanden wurde, erklärt die ungewöhnliche Höhe des Schalenbrunnens, der sich aus der Ferne wie ein konkurrierender kristallener »Wasser-Baum« vor der grünen Laubwand abhebt. Mit außerordentlicher Sensibilität haben Lenné und Fintelmann diesen überreich strömenden Schalenbrunnen mit der Parkanlage verbunden. Mehrfach ist das glitzernde Wasser Blickpunkt von Durchsichten, ohne daß ein Weg erkennbar dorthin führen würde. Erst wenn das Rauschen des Wassers schon vernehmbar wird, ziehen kreisende Wege den Spaziergänger in den ruhenden runden Raum der Wasserkunst. Sonnenlicht bricht sich in dem zweifachen »Wassermantel«, dessen Rauschen unter den hohen Bäumen an einen Monsunregen erinnert, während zugleich der feine Wasserstaub die Luft belebt und erfrischt. Rom und das tropische Tahiti werden hier noch einmal in indirekter Anspielung aufgerufen. Friedrich Schleiermacher nutzte die Bewässerungsanlagen der Insel in seinen 1832/33 gehaltenen Vorlesungen über die Ästhetik zu folgender Betrachtung: »Die schönen Gartenanlagen der Pfaueninsel bei Potsdam sind als Insel rings von Wasser umgeben, und doch hat sie erst ihre Vollkommenheit erreicht, indem eine künstliche Bewässerung hinzutritt, die durch eine besondere Maschine beschafft wird. Hierin zeigt sich erst das Hinreichende für die Erhaltung des vegetativen Lebens in seiner Steigerung, und wo es gänzlich daran fehlt, wird man es durchaus nicht zu einiger Vollkommenheit bringen ...«[32]

Der Abbruch eines spätgotischen Hauses in der Danziger Brotbänkengasse im Jahr 1823 war Anlaß, das

19. Die Fontäne auf der Pfaueninsel. Ölgemälde von Theodor Krüger, um 1840. (Stiftung Schlösser und Gärten Potsdam-Sanssouci, Fotoarchiv)

19. The Fountain on the Pfaueninsel. Oil painting by Theodeor Krüger, c. 1840. (Stiftung Schlösser und Gärten Potsdam-Sanssouci, Fotoarchiv)

edges of this axis. Constructions for the Menagerie began to be built in 1824 and they eventually included a cage for eagles, an ape house, an aviary and a house for exotic waterfowl located in a man-made pond; additionally, a Gothic pheasant-house that had stood in the Neuer Garten was also brought over to the island and enlarged.

It was also around 1824 that a self-contained, circular flower garden, with concentric paths and beds, was laid out between the Steward's House and the Castle, in the area once taken up by the animal cages. Here, in the so-called Round Garden the most beautiful flowers of the season are arranged in tiers – not unlike a theatre – and they give the garden its distinctive character. An arbour at the edge of this garden allows for an undisturbed view of these flower circles. Now and then a peacock will appear on this tranquil scene. Concurrent with the construction of the Menagerie buildings was the installation of an artificial irrigation system. This was the first garden in Brandenburg where such a system became a permanent fixture. A solidly-built house – where the talented machinist also lived – was constructed for this purpose on the island's southern shore. It contained an English steam-driven engine which conducted river water into a round reservoir located at the island's highest point. The technical requirements were given artistic expression by placing a cast-iron Roman-style well into the tank and having all of the water in the tank pour over its basin. This occurred for the first time on the monarch's birthday on 3 August 1825, and he was present to witness the event. Because the Fountain resembles the candlesticks of antiquity, it was commonly known as a »candelabrum«. This was also an apt description of the water's illuminative quality. The Fountain's unusual height is explained by the fact that when it was installed it was surrounded by tall, gnarled oak trees. From a distance, it stands out against the green wall of foliage like a rival, crystalline »water tree«. Lenné and Fintelmann were highly sensitive to the relationship between the Fountain with its lavish overflow and the surrounding park. The glistening water can be seen from many different points, even when there does not seem to be a path that leads to it. It is only when one can actually hear the water, that circular paths pull one towards the calm, round space containing the Fountain. Sunlight is refracted by the double »water coat«, which rustles under the tall tress like a monsoon rainfall, while the fine spray brightens and freshens the air. Here, once again, an indirect allusion is made to Rome and tropical Tahiti. In a series of lectures on aesthetics (1832/33), Friedrich Schleier-macher used the island's irrigation facilities to make the following point: »The beautiful gardens on the Pfaueninsel are surrounded by water, and yet their potential could only be fully developed by artificial irrigation, made possible by a machine. It is through such measures that the qualities of vegetative life can be heightened. If these are lacking, the full development of such qualities cannot occur...«[32]

The demolition of a late Gothic house in Danzig in 1823 was the impetus for a renewed staging of Gothic architecture on the island. Although the aim this time was to preserve an authentic piece of Gothic architecture, what resulted was still peculiar and new. On Schinkel's suggestion, the Danzig façade was placed in front of the southern tower of the Guest House, built in 1803/04. This meant that the tower had to be completely rebuilt and a storey added to the Guest House. Schinkel was very sparing in his use of ornamentation for the Guest House and his variations were clearly distinct from those of the original Gothic façade. This long building with its two towers thereby took on the appearance of an English country seat. Its »castellated style« has been familiar ever since Humphry Repton's *Red Books*. The relocation of the façade from Danzig to the Pfaueninsel was not yet sufficiently evocative for the era's romantic spirit. The rumour circulated that the façade had originated in Venice and then graced Nuremberg, the German medieval city par excellence.[33] The unreal, dreamlike quality, always a feature of the island, thereby took on a further variation.

Thema Gotik auf der Insel erneut zu inszenieren, dies-
mal zuförderst authentisch und in denkmalpflegeri-
scher Absicht. Dennoch entstand etwas eigentümlich
Neues daraus. Auf Schinkels Vorschlag wurde die
Danziger Fassade dem südlichen Turm des Kavalierhauses von 1803/04 vorgeblendet. De facto mußte jedoch dieser Turm mit der alten Fassade von Grund auf
neu errichtet werden. Schinkel schmückte das Übrige
des um ein Stockwerk erhöhten Kavalierhauses auffällig sparsam und mit deutlich von dem originalen gotischen Fassadendekor abweichenden Variationen. Das
langgestreckte zweitürmige Gebäude erhielt so das
Aussehen eines englischen Landsitzes im »castellated
style«, wie man ihn aus den *Red Books* von Humphry
Repton kennt. Der zeitgenössischen romantischen
Fama war die Translozierung der Fassade von Danzig
zur Pfaueninsel noch nicht beziehungsreich genug,
und sie behauptete daher, daß sie zuvor ihren Weg
vom Ursprung Venedig über Nürnberg, die deutsche
Stadt des Mittelalters schlechthin, genommen habe.[33]
Das Unwirklich-Traumhafte, das der Insel zuvor schon
anhaftete, fand mit dieser Legende nur seine Fortset-
zung.
Nach 1828 wurde die Menagerie um eine Bärengrube,
ein Känguruhhaus und Ställe für Wölfe, Füchse sowie
chinesische und brasilianische Schweine vermehrt.
Lenné rückte diese Bauten in großzügiger Streuung in
Gehölznischen zu beiden Seiten einer die Insel im Süden durchziehenden Sichtachse, die, in der Mitte in
stumpfem Winkel gebrochen, von den Enden her gesehen in dieser Mitte verdämmert. Von dem am Wasservogelteich liegenden Brechpunkt jedoch ist der
Blick nach Westen zum Schloß und nach Osten zum
fernen Havelberg mit der davorgelagerten Insel
Schwanenwerder offen. Die Tiergehege traten in der
Parklandschaft kaum in Erscheinung und ordneten
sich entschieden den großen Raumstrukturen unter.
Sie wurden nur einzeln und jeweils bei der Annäherung
wahrgenommen.

1829 ersetzte man den Sandsteinportikus des Luisen-
mausoleums in Charlottenburg durch eine Kopie aus
rotem Granit. Da die Absicht, der Verewigten auf der
Insel ein Erinnerungsmonument zu stiften, schon seit
ihrem Tod bestand, ergriff man diese Gelegenheit und
brachte das Sandsteinoriginal hierher und erweiterte
es zu einer Gedächtnishalle. Ganz angemessen wählte
man für dieses Bauwerk eine künstliche Bodenaufwöl-
bung am südlichen Waldrand des Meiereigebiets, also
in dem Bereich der Insel, der als einziger sein Aussehen seit den Tagen der Königin nicht verändert hatte.
Zu beiden Seiten dieses Tempels wachsen ehrwürdige
»vaterländische« Eichen. Ihrer Bestimmung angemessen ist die immer schattige Halle nach Norden gerichtet, und die vier dorischen Säulen streift nur zu früher
oder später Stunde flüchtiges Sonnenlicht.
Mit dem Bau des Palmenhauses für die in Paris erwor-
bene Sammlung großer Palmen erreichte die Entwicklung der Insel ihren Höhepunkt. Albert Dietrich Schadow führte den Bau 1830/31 nach Schinkels Entwurf
aus. Dieses im Äußeren ganz funktionale Haus überraschte im Inneren, indisch-islamisch dekoriert, mit
exotischer Pracht. Auf die an anderer Stelle ausgebrei-
tete Baugeschichte kann hier nicht eingegangen werden.[34] Alexander von Humboldt setzte dem Palmenhaus in seinem *Kosmos* mit der Feststellung ein Denk-
mal, daß es neben dem von Loddiges in London eine
fast authentische Vorstellung der Tropen böte.[35] Seit
1810 kultivierte Fintelmann eingedenk der im Otaheitischen Kabinett postulierten Schwesternschaft der
Pfaueninsel zu den Inseln der Südsee hier Blattpflanzen, Symbole des Tropischen schlechthin. Die Pfaueninsel wurde damit zur Wiege der Blattpflanzenmode
des 19. Jahrhunderts. Im Palmenhaus erfuhr das Ta-
hiti-Motiv der Pfaueninsel seine orientalische Variante.
Nach der Südsee galt an der Wende vom 18. zum 19.
Jahrhundert das Interesse Europas, insbesondere
Englands, dem fernen Orient. Im Winter 1821 hatte der
Berliner Hof die orientalische Romanze *Lalla Rookh*

24. Blick von der Pfaueninsel zum Havelberg, links der
Wolfsstall. Ausschnitt aus einem Panoramabild auf einer
Porzellanvase im Schloß Kalkum, 1833. (Nordrhein-
Westfälisches Hauptstaatsarchiv, Düsseldorf)
25. Albert Dietrich Schadow, »Project zur Erbauung ei-
nes Stalles für die Känguhru«, 1828. (Verwaltung der
Schlösser und Gärten Berlin, Pk 2054)

24. View from the Pfaueninsel onto the Havelberg, on
the left the Stall for Wolves. Detail from a panoramic
view on a porcelain vase in Schloß Kalkum, 1833.
(Nordrhein-Westfälisches Hauptstaatsarchiv,
Düsseldorf)
25. Albert Dietrich Schadow, »Project for the construction of a kangaroo house«, 1828. (Verwaltung der Staatlichen Schlösser und Gärten Berlin, Pk 2054)

The Menagerie was enlarged after 1828. The additions included a bear-pit, a kangaroo house, and stalls that housed wolves, foxes and Chinese and Brazilian pigs. Lenné placed these constructions at a generous distance from each other in openings in the copse. They were located on both sides of a visual axis that ran through the southern part of the island. This axis is broken by an obtuse angle at its centre. Indeed, when the axis is viewed from its ends it seems to fade away at its centre. Yet it is at this point – where the pond for the waterfowl is also located – that one enjoys an unobstructed view. To the west one can see the Castle and to the east, in the distance, is the Havelberg with the island of Schwanenwerder in front of it. The animal compounds were barely visible in the park landscape and were completely subordinate to the larger spatial structures. They were only noticed as individual constructions when one stood close to them.

In 1829 the sandstone portico in front of Queen Luise's Mausoleum in Charlottenburg was replaced by a copy made of red granite. Ever since her death, there had been plans to erect a memorial to the queen on the Pfaueninsel and the opportunity was now seized. The sandstone original was brought to the island and expanded into a memorial hall. The building was placed on an artificial elevation at the southern edge of the forest belonging to the Dairy area. This was an appropriate choice since this part of the island had not changed its appearance since the queen's death. The temple is flanked by the »fatherland's« oak trees. As befits a temple, it faces north and is always shady. It is only very early or very late in the day that fleeting sunlight touches the four Doric columns.

The architectural development of the island reached a high point with the construction of a building to house a collection of large palm trees that had been purchased in Paris. The Palm House was realized between 1830/31 under the direction of Albert Dietrich Schadow, according to a design by Schinkel. From the outside, this building seems completely functional, and the exotic splendour of its interior, with its Indian and Islamic ornamentation, comes as a surprise. The background to its construction has already been described elsewhere.[34] Alexander von Humboldt lavished high praise on the Palm House in his work *Kosmos*. Apart from Loddiges' Palm House in London, he considered it to be the only such structure that provided an almost authentic impression of the tropics.[35] The Otaheite Cabinet had already postulated a sister

hood between the Pfaueninsel and the South Sea Islands. With this in mind, Fintelmann had cultivated foliage plants – epitomes of the tropics – since 1810. The Pfaueninsel thereby became one of the sources of the fashion for foliage plants that developed in the 19th century. In the Palm House the island's Tahiti motif took on an Oriental variation. In the late 18th and early 19th century the Far East attracted a great deal of interest in Europe, particularly in England. In the winter of 1821 Berlin's royal court had presented tableaux vivants taken from *Lalla Rookh*, a narrative poem with an Oriental setting by the Irish poet Thomas Moore. A year later Gaspare Spontini used this material for the opera *Nurmahal oder das Rosenfest von Kaschmir* for which Schinkel did the stage design. These events, as well as the inspiring genius loci of the Pfaueninsel, were the catalysts leading to the creation of the Rose Garden and the Indian Palm House. The site chosen for the Palm House lay in the copse to the north of the Castle. A reciprocal relationship was thereby established between the rose labyrinthe lying on the hill to the south of the Castle, the soft curve of the meadow on which the Castle stands and the transparent Indian fairy palace. The Palm House was 34 m long and 10 m high. A path already existed that would have allowed for a virtually frontal approach to this cubic building. Instead, this path was not only shifted to the side of the building, it was also connected to one of the pergolas that were themselves a link to the surrounding park. Such measures reveal the sensitivity of the underlying landscaping concept for the island. The area around the Palm House was given a special atmosphere through the exclusive cultivation of green foliage. The royal gardener for the Pfaueninsel, Gustav Adolph Fintelmann, considered these plants to be reminders of the »distant tropics, where we so often long to be; there, where vegetation rules in all its splendour«.[36]

The Palm House was destroyed by fire in 1880. This important component in the overall impression of the island was thereby lost forever. Two pedestals that escaped the flames today mark the dimensions of this building. As they are an important element for understanding the context, the foliage plants that surrounded the Palm House have been recultivated on the basis of the decription of 1837.[37]

It is not possible here to describe the inhabitants of the island and their interesting backgrounds. An exception must be made, however, for Harry Maitey, a native of the Sandwich Isles, who began to work for

des irischen Dichters Thomas Moore in lebenden Bildern aufgeführt. Ein Jahr später formte Gaspare Spontini diesen Stoff zur Oper *Nurmahal oder das Rosenfest von Kaschmir*, für die Schinkel die Bühnenbilder schuf. Ursächlich waren es dieses Erlebnis und die Inspiration durch den Genius loci der Pfaueninsel, die zur Anlage des Rosengartens und zum Bau des indischen Palmenhauses den Anstoß gaben. Als Bauplatz für das Palmenhaus wählte man den nördlichen Gehölzrand der Schloßwiese. Dadurch trat das im Süden auf dem Hügel ruhende Rosenlabyrinth über die sanft geschwungene Schloßwiese hinweg mit dem in der Gehölzkulisse stehenden gläsernen indischen Feenpalast in wechselseitige Korrespondenz. Wie sensibel die gärtnerische Gesamtkomposition auf jede Veränderung reagierte, zeigt sich daran, daß man einen bestehenden Weg, der beinahe frontal auf den 34m langen und 10m hohen Kubus des Palmenhauses führte, so verlegte, daß er sich nun diesem Baukörper von einer der beiden Seiten, die durch angesetzte Pergolen in die Parklandschaft eingebunden wurden, näherte. Die Umgebung des Palmenhauses erhielt ihre besondere Atmosphäre durch die ausschließliche Verwendung von Blattpflanzen, die nach Überzeugung des Pfaueninsel-Hofgärtners Gustav Adolph Fintelmann uns »an die fernen Tropen« mahnen, »wohin uns unsere Wünsche so oft tragen, dort, wo die Vegetation in ihrer ganzen Macht herrscht«.[36] Der Untergang des Palmenhauses durch ein Großfeuer im Jahr 1880 ist ein bleibender Verlust für das Gesamtbild der Insel. Heute markieren aus dem Brandschutt geborgene Postamente die Dimensionen des verlorenen Bauwerks. Die Blattpflanzengruppen aus der Umgebung des Hauses wurden nach der Beschreibung von 1837[37] als wesentliches Element zum Verständnis der Zusammenhänge wiederhergestellt.

In dieser Darstellung ist nicht Platz, auf die Inselbewohner und ihre interessanten Verhältnisse einzugehen. Als Ausnahme sei angemerkt, daß im ersten Baujahr des Palmenhauses der Sandwichinsulaner Harry Maitey Anstellung beim Maschinenmeister Friedrich auf der Pfaueninsel fand. Maitey hatte Ende 1823, als

das der Preußischen Seehandlung gehörende Schiff »Mentor« vor der Insel Oahu (bekannt durch den Ort Honolulu) ankerte, »freiwillig die Aufnahme zur Mit-Reise begehrt«. Ende 1824 gelangte Maitey nach Berlin und kam in die Obhut des Präsidenten der Seehandlung, Rother. Rother kümmerte sich um Unterricht in Sprache und Christentum, und so konnte Maitey 1830 im Alter von 22 oder 23 Jahren getauft werden. Da sich der Sohn Hawaiis wegen unzureichender Kenntnisse der Chargen und Titulaturen nicht zu dem ihm zugedachten Posten als Kanzleibote eignete, wurde er zur Ausbildung und als Hilfe dem Maschinenmeister Friedrich zugeteilt. Er soll großen Anteil an der Herstellung der bekannten Architekturmodelle seines Lehrers gehabt haben. Maitey durfte 1833 Dorothea Charlotte Becker, Tochter des Pfaueninsel-Tierpflegers, heiraten. Wie selbstverständlich steuerte Maitey als königlicher Angestellter dem Personal der Insel eine exotische Komponente bei. Die Eltern seiner Frau waren sich der Auszeichnung, Schwiegereltern eines Sandwichinsulaners zu sein, wohl bewußt und ließen das auf ihrem noch erhaltenen Grabstein vermerken.[38]

Die durch das Palmenhaus bedingte vermehrte Pflege der Insel erforderte ein neues Wohnhaus für Gärtner und anderes Personal. Es entstand nach einem Entwurf von Schinkel 1829/30 als »Schweizerhaus«. Wie immer auf der Pfaueninsel, mußte der dafür angemessene Ort im Gartenraum sorgfältig ausgewählt werden. Der wohl von Lenné angegebene Platz auf dem hohen Ufer zwischen Schloß und Kastellanhaus genügt der Bedingung, diesen beiden Gebäuden nahe zu sein, aber dennoch ist der Schinkelbau von ihnen durch eine dichte Abpflanzung und geschickte Wegeführung völlig getrennt und empfängt die ihm notwendige landschaftliche Ergänzung und Weite, indem er sich zur Havel und der jenseitigen Höhe von Nikolskoe mit Blockhaus und Kirche öffnet. Benutzt man den im Bogen vom Kastellanhaus heraufführenden Weg, so erblickt man beim Ansteigen zuerst die reiche südliche Giebelfront des Hauses. Erfaßt das Auge dann die Westfassade mit dem tief eingeschnittenen Eingang, so verbindet sich mit diesem Eindruck das Erlebnis

28. Karl Friedrich Schinkel, das Schweizerhaus auf der Pfaueninsel, 1829. (Verwaltung der Schlösser und Gärten Berlin, Fotoarchiv)
29. Das Innere des Palmenhauses auf der Pfaueninsel. Ölgemälde von Karl Blechen, 1834. (Stiftung Schlösser und Gärten Potsdam-Sanssouci, GK I 4054)

28. Karl Friedrich Schinkel, the Swiss House on the Pfaueninsel, 1829. (Verwaltung der Staatlichen Schlösser und Gärten Berlin, Fotoarchiv)
29. The interior of the Palm House on the Pfaueninsel. Oil painting by Karl Blechen, 1834. (Stiftung Schlösser und Gärten Potsdam-Sanssouci, GK I 4054)

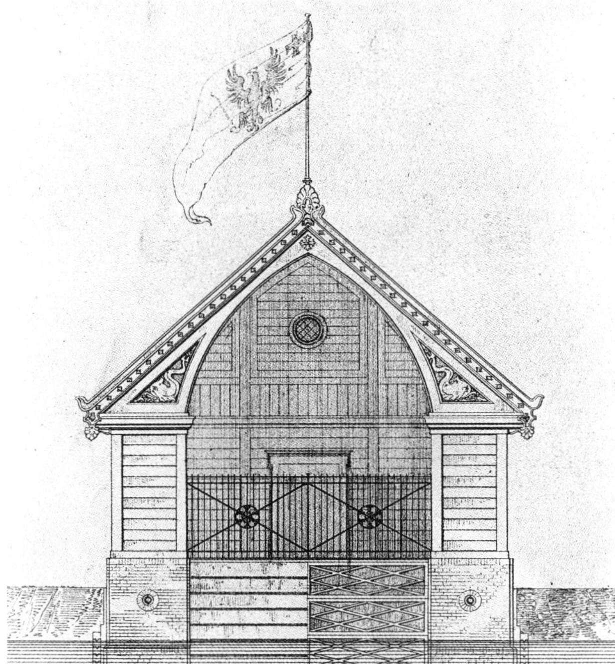

the machine minder Friedrich in the year that construction began on the Palm House. In 1823 when the ship »Mentor«, owned by the Preußische Seehandlung, was anchored on the island of Oahu (the site of Honolulu) Maitey »requested of his own free will to be taken along«. After arriving in Berlin at the end of 1824, he was taken under the wing of the president of the Seehandlung, Rother, who saw that he was instructed in reading, writing and Christianity. In 1830, at the age of either 22 or 23, Maitey was baptized. Although it was originally foreseen that he would be employed as a messenger boy, his insufficient knowledge of ranks and titles brought this plan to nought. He was sent to the machine minder on the Pfaueninsel, Friedrich, and was trained as his helper. He is said to have played an important role in the creation of his teacher's well-known architectural models. In 1833 he was permitted to marry Dorothea Charlotte Becker, the daughter of the zoo-keeper on the Pfaueninsel. Employed by the king, Maitey was certainly an exotic presence amongst the island's staff. His wife's parents considered it to be such an honour to have a native of the Sandwich Isles as their son-in-law, that they had this distinction engraved on their (still existent) gravestone.[38]

Once the Palm House was completed, the island's maintenance requirements also increased and new quarters for gardeners and staff were needed. These were built in 1829/30, according to a design by Schinkel and would be known as the Swiss House. As was always the case with new buildings on the island, the site for this house had to be very carefully chosen. It was probably Lenné who decided that it should be placed on the shore, between the Castle and the Steward's House. Despite its close proximity to these buildings, thick shrubbery and skilfully laid out paths ensured that it was also completely separate from them. The house was also given the necessary scenic breadth and scope through a view that opens up over the Havel and onto Nikolskoe, with its log-cabin and church. If one climbs up the curved path leading from the Steward's House, one will first see this house's southern gabled front. The western façade, with its entrance carved deep into the wood, comes into view simultaneously with one's awareness of the altitude and the expanse of landscape opening up to the left. It is because of its altitude and this free expanse of landscape that this site differs from any other place on the island. The veneration of nature and of a life free of society's corruptions had been a tradition on the island since the development of the Tahitian allegory, and the Swiss House should be understood as a continuation of this tradition. Albrecht von Haller's poem »The Alps«, Jean Jacques Rousseau's celebration of the Alpine nature and Friedrich von Schiller's *Wilhelm Tell* had helped to create the idea that, here, in the heart of Europe, was a land of exemplary natural and social structures. To this point the Swiss farmhouse had not elicited much architectural attention but Schinkel now saw in it the basic architectonic principle of the Greek temple. This is why the ascent from the Steward's House to the Swiss House can also be understood in programmatic terms. Proceeding from the garden path, the ascent leads from a naive conception of a farmhouse (the Steward's House) to the rural prototype of Greek architecture (the Swiss House).

In 1830 the island's most impressive animal shelter was built according to a design by Schadow. Located in the copse at the entrance to the Menagerie, it was only 250 steps away from the Sol fountain. This house for llamas and cockatoos was fashioned in the Italian villa style of the Schinkel school and combined elements of the Palazzo Caprini (»Raphael's House«) and the Casa Cenci. Partially destroyed by fire in 1842, the building was completely demolished in 1870. All that remains is a round basin which spouts water and which once lay in the animal compound. It is still known today as the »Llama Fountain«.

A miniature frigate that had been a gift of the English monarch in 1814 did not survive the ravages of Brandenburg's winters. As a replacement, in 1832 a second frigate was sent from England. Schadow built a winter harbour for it at the foot of the island's steep southern shore. In the summer this construction resembles an architectonically rendered entrance to a water grotto and thereby adds a further element to the island's many motifs.

der Höhenlage und der sich links öffnenden landschaftlichen Weite, das diesen Ort gänzlich von der übrigen Insel absondert. Das Schweizerhaus setzt die zu Anfang mit dem Tahiti-Gleichnis auf der Insel begonnene Tradition der Verehrung von Naturnähe und gesellschaftlicher Unverdorbenheit fort. Galt doch die Schweiz durch Albrecht von Hallers Gedicht »Die Alpen«, Jean Jacques Rousseaus Verherrlichung der Alpennatur oder Friedrich von Schillers *Wilhelm Tell* als ein Muster natürlicher und sozialer Lebensform im Herzen Europas. Schinkel erkannte in dem zuvor kaum geachteten Schweizer Bauernhaus das architektonische Grundprinzip des griechischen Tempels. So läßt sich der durch den Gartenweg vorgegebene Aufstieg vom Kastellanhaus, als dem Ausdruck einer naiven Auffassung des Bauernhauses, zum Schweizerhaus, als dem ländlichen Urbild griechischer Architektur, auch als Programm verstehen.

1830 entstand nach Schadows Entwurf am Eingang zum Menageriebereich, in die Gehölzmasse gebettet, das edelste der Tierhäuser der Insel. 250 Schritt vom Jacobsbrunnen entfernt, wurde im italienischen Villenstil der Schinkelschule ein Haus für Lamas und Kakadus errichtet, das in sich Elemente der beiden Vorbilder, des Palazzo Caprini (»Haus Raffaels«) und der Casa Cenci, vereinte. Das 1842 durch Feuer teilzerstörte Gebäude wurde 1870 abgetragen. Nur das einst im Gehege gelegene runde Becken mit Springstrahl gibt heute noch als »Lamabrunnen« Kunde von dem untergegangenen Bau.

Eine vom englischen König 1814 als Geschenk empfangene Miniaturfregatte hatte den Unbilden der brandenburgischen Winter ohne Schutz nicht standgehalten. Für die als Ersatz im Jahr 1832 aus England gesandte zweite Fregatte erbaute Schadow einen Winterhafen am Fuß des steilen Südufers der Insel. Im Sommer wirkt dieses Bauwerk wie die architektonisch gefaßte Einfahrt zu einer Wassergrotte und fügt somit der Vielzahl der Inselmotive ein weiteres Element hinzu.

Das Ergebnis des vorangegangenen Gestaltungsprozesses zeigt der von Gerhard Koeber 1834 gezeichnete Plan mit der unvermeidbaren Grobheit und Unzulänglichkeit, die ein Plan gegenüber der Gartenwirklichkeit leider hat. Die generalisierende Sprache dieses Planes findet ihre notwendige Ergänzung in dem von Fintelmann 1828 mit subtiler Kenntnis der Baumgestalten gefertigten Plan. Es sei noch einmal an das eingangs Gesagte erinnert, daß sich das komplexe System der auf der modellierten Erdoberfläche sanft schwingenden Wege in seinem Verhältnis zu den Gartenräumen und Gebäuden der genauen Beschreibung und verständlichen zeichnerischen Darstellung entzieht. Die Insel gliedert sich ohne trennende Zäsur in drei Zonen oder Bereiche:

das Gebiet um die Große Schloßwiese mit den Schmuckanlagen am Schloß, dem Runden Garten, dem Rosengarten und dem Bereich der Blattpflanzen und exotischen Gewächse am Palmenhaus;

den hainartigen Menageriebereich in der Inselmitte mit den beiden durchlaufenden Sichtachsen;

den Ostteil der Insel mit seinen von Gehölzen umsäumten drei Ackerflächen und den offenen Wiesen

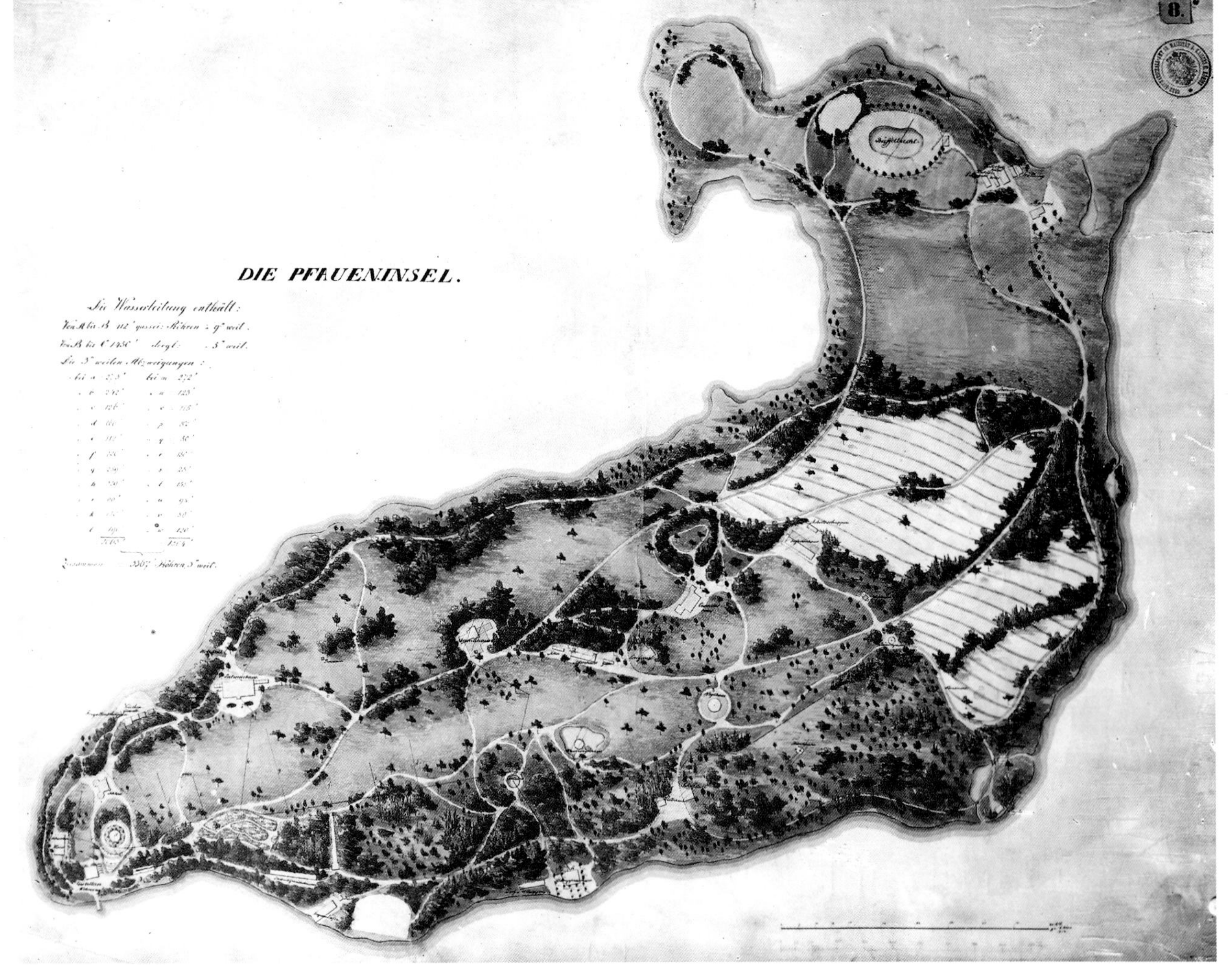

32. Plan der Pfaueninsel. Aquarellierte Federzeichnung von Gerhard Koeber, 1834. Die Angaben über die Wasserleitungen wurden um 1870 eingetragen. (Verwaltung der Staatlichen Schlösser und Gärten Berlin, Fotoarchiv)
33. Luftbild der Pfaueninsel, Mai 1992. (Senatsverwaltung für Bau- und Wohnungswesen Berlin, Abt. V, Nr. 538/93)

32. Plan of the Pfaueninsel. Pen-and-wash drawing by Gerhard Koeber, 1834. The data on the water pipes was entered c. 1870. (Verwaltung der Staatlichen Schlösser und Gärten Berlin, Fotoarchiv)
33. Aerial view of the Pfaueninsel, May 1992. (Senatsverwaltung für Bau- und Wohnungswesen Berlin, Abt. V, Nr. 538/93)

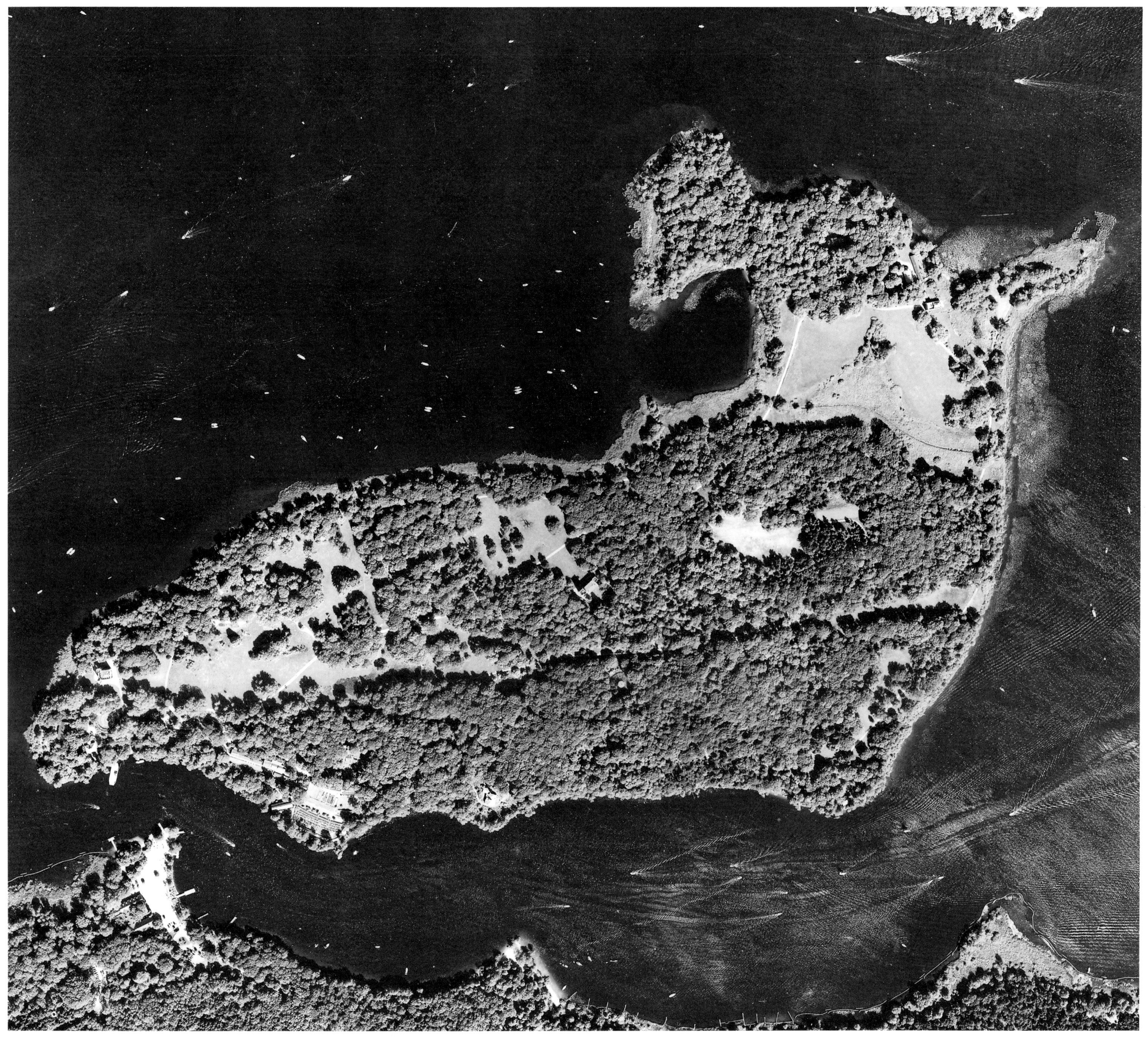

der Meierei, der seinen Charakter aus der Periode der »ferme ornée« mit nur geringfügigen Änderungen bewahrt hat.

Ganz unterschiedlich ist die Behandlung von Außenansicht und Innenraum der Insel. Der Anblick der Ufer vom Wasser blieb immer abwehrend, durch Bäume oder steile Böschungen verstellt; das Ufer wurde nie gestaltet und konserviert im Gegensatz zu anderen Gärten Lennés etwas von der geheimnisvollen, autonomen Wildnis des Ursprungs. Um so überraschender erscheint dann das lichte, weite, vielgestaltige Innere. Noch beim Betreten der Insel, als Kastellan- oder am Fährhaus, empfängt den Besucher schlichte Ländlichkeit, die nichts von dem vorwegnimmt, was die Insel in märchenhaftem Verborgensein an Überraschungen bereithält. Es gilt, was Alexandre de Laborde, Nicolas Boileau-Despréaux' Maxime von der Dichtung auf den Garten übertragend, vom Eingang zum Landschaftsgarten Méréville sagte: »Que le début soit simple et n'ait rien d'affecté.«[39] Hat man das Plateau der Insel erreicht, so entwickelt sich mit jedem Schritt, dank der spannungsreich zur Bodenbewegung und zu den Gartenräumen geführten Wege, ein stets vorwärts lockender Fluß der Bilder. Zwei große Sichtachsen, die Große Sicht und die Menagerieachse, durchziehen die Insel in Ostwestrichtung. Von der ersteren öffnen sich immer wieder neue Nebenräume zum Flußtal hin. Keine Wegekurve ist zufällig, sondern rückt immer wechselnde Ziele ins Blickfeld oder hebt und senkt den Horizont. In dieses dynamische Spiel sind in sich ruhende Sonderräume eingefügt: der Runde Blumengarten, der Rosengarten, das Fontänenrund und der Palmenhausplatz. Ein zentraler Erlebnisraum ist die Große Schloßwiese, die, selbst fast leer, Fokus der »Idee«[40] der Insel ist. Ihre Aussage verdichtet sich beim Gang über den Zedernweg, das heißt, nur die Bewegung auf diesem Weg erschließt in dichter Folge diese Eindrücke. Im Westen faßt der Blick auf die weite Wasserfläche, an dem diagonal gestellten Schloß vorbei, die Tahiti-Anspielung und den empfindsam-sentimentalen Ursprung der eigenen Geschichtlichkeit der Insel zusammen. Im Norden und Süden liegen sich, wie schon ausführlicher beschrieben, Indischer Palast und Rosenlabyrinth gegenüber. Auf der Ostseite werden die Unendlichkeit und das Naturschöne durch die beiden Sichtachsen aufgerufen. An Vergänglichkeit und zugleich die Kraft des Überdauerns gemahnen die Eichenruinen am Rand der Meiereiachse. Dazwischen zeigt sich fern auf sanft ansteigendem Hügel, in Grün gehüllt, das glitzernd strömende Wasser der Fontäne in Opposition zum ruhenden Spiegel der Havel: Wasser als Symbol des Kreislaufs alles Lebendigen und zugleich als Seele und tatsächlich genutzte Quelle des Gartens.

Nach dem Tod Friedrich Wilhelms III. im Jahr 1840 erfuhr die Insel keine weitere künstlerische Entwicklung, lediglich dem Palmenhaus wurde 1845 die schon ursprünglich geplante gläserne Zwiebelkuppel aufgesetzt. Es lag wohl in der Absicht Friedrich Wilhelms IV., des künstlerisch hochbegabten Nachfolgers, die Insel als Zeugnis der Zeit seines Vaters und der eigenen Jugend zu bewahren und als Gesamtkunstwerk zu konservieren. Der sensible König mochte gespürt haben, daß die allzu zoologisch und publikumswirksam gewordene Menagerie in sich die Tendenz zur Verselbständigung trug und somit eine Gefahr für das Kunstwerk Pfaueninsel wurde. Darum wurde 1842 die Menagerie aufgelöst und dem damals gegründeten Berliner Zoo überwiesen. Nur das Wasservogelhaus und die Voliere verblieben der Insel. Der »Verlust« der Menagerie war aufs Ganze gesehen ein Gewinn für die Insel. Um drohende wirtschaftliche Ausbeutung zu verhindern, wurde die Pfaueninsel 1924 unter Naturschutz gestellt, da es den Denkmalschutz für Gärten zu dieser Zeit noch nicht gab. Mangelnde Pflege während der Kriegszeit und der ersten Nachkriegsjahre hatte das Zuwachsen von Sichtbeziehungen, einen Gestaltverlust der Gartenräume und die Verlagerung zahlreicher Wege zur Folge. Da die Insel von starken Eingriffen in das Bodengefüge verschont blieb, lassen sich diese Schäden in sukzessiver gartendenkmalpflegerischer Arbeit beheben.

Es scheint fast paradox, daß die Pfaueninsel unter dem nüchtern-realistischen König Friedrich Wilhelm III. ihre Blüte und Vollendung erreichte. Aus den phantastischen Veduten des willensschwachen Friedrich Wilhelm II. entwickelte sich ein Gesamtkunstwerk, in dem die Inspirationen der ersten Anlage sichtbar blieben und zugleich weitergesponnen wurden. Dem naiven und fast aufdringlichen Umgang mit Gefühl und Mystik unter Friedrich Wilhelm II. folgte der aufgeklärte, ästhetisch vollkommene Stil Lennés, in dem Anspielungen und Zwischentöne wie in einem Roman Theodor Fontanes zurückhaltend und elegant verschlüsselt sind.

While Gerhard Koeber's plan of 1834 depicts the changes that were undertaken on the island between 1816 and 1834, it inevitably seems coarse and inadequate when it is compared with the reality of the garden. The necessary augmentation to this plan's generalizations can be found in Fintelmann's plan of 1828 in which he displays his intensive knowledge of the island's trees. At this point, however, it must be reiterated, that neither words nor drawings can adequately describe the complex system of softly curving paths that run over the island's modelled surface or their relationships to the garden and the buildings. Although there is no clear separation between them, the island can be divided into three zones or areas:

the expanse around the large meadow on which the Castle stands including the Castle's decorative installations, the Round Garden, the Rose Garden and the area with the foliage and exotic plants at the Palm House;

the grove-like area for the Menagerie in the middle of the island, with its two uninterrupted visual axes;

the eastern part of the island with its three arable areas bordered by copses and the open meadows of the Dairy which has remained virtually unchanged since its »ferme ornée« period.

The »outside view« of the island must be understood in different terms than its interior spaces. The view of the shore from the water was always shielded, obstructed by trees or steep banks. In contrast to Lenné's other gardens, the Pfaueninsel shoreline was never shaped in any way and it thereby preserved something of its original mysterious and autonomous wildness. This is why the island's bright, broad and multifarious interior comes as a particular surprise. Indeed, even when one has already landed on the island and is standing at the Steward's House or the Ferry House, the simple rural atmosphere gives no hint of the surprises that the island has hidden away, like treasures in a fairy tale. Alexander de Laborde once applied Nicolas Boileau-Despréaux's poetic maxim to the entrance of the landscape garden of Méréville, and the same could also be done for the Pfaueninsel: »Que le début soit simple et n'ait rien d'affecté.«[39] Once one has reached the island's plateau and is walking along the paths running over the ground's different contours and leading to the garden areas, visual impressions flow past and seem to propel one ever forward. Two large visual axes, the »Grand View« and the »Menagerie Axis« run through the island in an east-west direction. The first axis is constantly augmented by new »adjoining« rooms facing the river valley. There are no coincidental curves in the island's paths. Each one provides a different view or raises and lowers the horizon. Woven into this constantly changing fabric are special, self-contained spaces such as the Round Garden, the Rose Garden, the circular Fountain area, and the Palm House area. The large, almost empty meadow on which the castle stands plays a central role in one's perceptions of the island. Its is itself the focus of the »idea«[40] of the island. Its significance becomes particularly apparent when one walks alongs its cedar path, for it is only by moving along this path that a series of impressions will follow in close succession upon each other. If one looks to the west, beyond the diagonally positioned Castle, one sees the broad expanse of water and recalls the allusions to Tahiti and the Romantic origins of the island's history. In the north and south, the Indian palace and the rose labyrinthe lie opposite each other in the dynamic relationship that has already been described. On the island's eastern side the two visual axes offer views of nature's beauties, as well as evoking a sense of boundlessness. The ruined oaks at the edge of the Dairy axis are reminders of the transitory character of natural phenomena but also of their power of survival. And, far away, on a gently sloping hill, wrapped in green, the glistening stream of the Fountain contrasts with the calm waters of the Havel. Water is here both the symbol of the cyclical nature of life and of the garden's soul and vital source.

After the death of Friedrich Wilhelm III in 1840 the artistic development of the island came to an end. Although a transparent onion dome was placed on top of the Palm House in 1845, this structure had always been foreseen for this building. The new monarch, Friedrich Wilhelm IV, was a man of great artistic sensibilties, and it was probably his intention to maintain the island as a reminder of his father's era and of his own youth and to conserve it as a synthesis of the arts. Over the years the Menagerie had taken on the qualities of a zoo and become a great favourite with the public. This sensitive monarch probably realized that the Menagerie's autonomous development was a threat to the Pfaueninsel as a work of art. In 1842 the Menagerie was dissolved and the animals donated to the recently established Berlin Zoo. Only the house for waterfowl and the Aviary remained on the island. The »loss« of the Menagerie was actually to the good of the island as a whole. Threatened by financial exploitation, the island was declared a nature reserve in 1924 (at this time the concept of monument preservation did not extend to gardens). As a result of insufficient care during the war and in the first years after the war, prospect points were overgrown, the garden configurations lost their contours and many paths were shifted. Nevertheless, because there were no major changes made in the structure of the island's ground surface, the damages outlined above can be successively rectified.

It seems almost a paradox that the island reached its full bloom and completion during the reign of such an earnest and pragmatic figure as Friedrich Wilhelm III. The fantastic views of the weak-willed Friedrich Wilhelm II became a synthesis of the arts in which the original inspiration remained visible but was at the same time also developed further. The naive and almost obtrusive attitude towards emotion and mysticism which prevailed under Friedrich Wilhelm II was followed by Lenné's enlighted and aesthetically mature style. Similar to the style of a novel by Theodor Fontane, the allusions and nuances are discreet and elegantly disguised.

Anmerkungen

[1] Fläche nach den 1992 abgeschlossenen Vermessungen. Die bisherige Angabe von 76 ha fußt noch auf der bei den Pachtverhandlungen im November 1793 vom Amt Bornstedt angegebenen Größe von etwa 300 preuß. Morgen = 76 ha.

[2] Martin Sperlich, »Eine römische Villa an der Havel«, in: Martin Sperlich und Michael Seiler, *Schloß und Park Glienicke*, 3. neugefaßte Auflage, Berlin 1987, S. 61.

[3] So bezeichnete auch der Dichter und Landschaftsgärtner (dieser Begriff wurde von ihm geprägt) William Shenstone (1714–1763) seinen von ihm verschönerten Landsitz The Leasowes.

[4] »Eine grosse landschaftliche Gartenanlage in meinem Sinne muß auf einer Grund-Idee beruhen. Sie muss mit Consequenz und, wenn sie ein gediegenes Kunstwerk werden soll, soviel als möglich nur von einer leitenden Hand angefangen und beendigt werden. Dieser Eine mag und soll die guten Gedanken vieler Anderer benutzen, er allein muss sie aber im Geiste zu einem Ganzen verarbeiten, damit der untrügliche Stempel der Individualität und Einheit nicht verloren gehe. Man verstehe mich indessen wohl: eine Grund-Idee, sage ich, soll dem Ganzen unterliegen, kein verworrenes Arbeiten aufs Gerathewohl statt finden, sondern der leitende durchbildende Gedanke auch an jedem Einzelnen zu erkennen seyn; und füglich mag dieser aus den speciellen Verhältnissen des Künstlers, aus den besonderen Umständen seines Lebens oder der früheren Geschichte seiner Familie entspringen, wie durch die Lokalität, welche er vorfindet, bedingt werden – aber damit verlange ich dennoch keinesweges, dass auch schon im Voraus der ganz genaue Plan der Ausführung bis in jedes *detail* entworfen, und daran streng gehalten werde. Grade das Gegentheil möchte ich in gewisser Hinsicht empfehlen; denn, sind auch mit der Idee die Hauptzüge des Ganzen vorher bestimmt, so soll doch während der Ausführung der Künstler sich ungezwungen den Inspirationen seiner Phantasie fortwährend überlassen, vielfach Neues auffinden, seinen Stoff im Schaffen immer noch fort studiren, namentlich hier die rohe vor ihm liegende Natur bei jeder verschiedenen Beleuchtung (denn mit schöner Beziehung ist das Licht eins seiner Haupt-Materiale) innerhalb und ausserhalb des Bezirks seiner kleinen Schöpfung beobachten, Ursache und Effect ergründen und hiernach die früheren, einzelnen Gedanken für das *detail* motiviren, oder auch theilweise gänzlich verlassen, wenn ihm später bessere Einsicht wird. Der Maler wird ja ebenfalls von Zeit und Zeit an seinem Gemälde, das doch so unendlich weniger mannichfaltig ist, dies und jenes ändern, diese Stellung gefälliger oder naturgemässer machen, hier eine Schattirung verbessern, dort jenem Zuge mehr Ausdruck geben müssen – wie wollte es dem Garten-Künstler, der mit so widerspenstigen und oft so schwer zu berechnenden Materialien arbeitet, und eine Menge verschiedene Bilder auch wiederum in eins vereinigen soll, gelingen, Alles auf den ersten Versuch unverbesserlich zu treffen!« Hermann Fürst von Pückler-Muskau, *Andeutungen über Landschaftsgärtnerei*, Nachdruck der Ausgabe von 1834, Stuttgart 1977, S. 18.

[5] Der Ursprung dieses Namens ist nicht geklärt, geht aber sicherlich nicht auf den Vogel Pfau zurück.

[6] Karl Breuer, *Die Pfaueninsel bei Potsdam*, maschinenschriftl. Dissertation der Technischen Hochschule Berlin, Berlin 1923, S. 138–145.

[7] Ebd., S. 179.

[8] *Voyage autour du monde, par la frégate du roi la Boudeuse, et la flute l'Étoile; en 1766, 1767, 1768 & 1769*, Paris 1771.

[9] *A voyage towards the South Pole and round the world*, London 1777.

[10] GStAPK, Abt. Merseburg, Acta des Kabinetts Friedrich Wilhelms II., S. 1.

[11] Carl Christian Horvath, *Potsdams Merkwürdigkeiten beschrieben und durch Plans und Prospekte erläutert*, Potsdam 1798, S. 222–236.

[12] Hermann Schmitz, *Das Marmorpalais bei Potsdam und das Schlößchen auf der Pfaueninsel*, Berlin 1921.

[13] Bertold Adolf Haase-Faulenorth, *Gräfin Lichtenau*, Berlin 1934, S. 26.

[14] Das tatsächlich am 28.4.1796 ausgefertigte Diplom wurde 2 Jahre zurückdatiert. Ebd., S. 195.

[15] Anm. 6, S. 36–46.

[16] Diese Vermutung spricht Karl Breuer in seiner Dissertation von 1923 aus. Anm. 6, S. 148, 149.

[17] SSGP, Sammlung der Inventare, Nr. 393.

[18] Auch Torre Mesa (Du Pérac 1575), Frontispizio di Nerone oder Templum Solis Aureliani genannt.

[19] Georg Forster, *Entdeckungsreise nach Tahiti und in die Südsee 1772–1775*, herausgegeben von Hermann Homann, Berlin 1989, S. 267, 269.

[20] Vgl. Anm. 3.

[21] Vgl. Norbert Miller, »Exkurs: Treppenhäuser – Raum als Einbildungskraft des Betrachters«, in: Norbert Miller, *Strawberry Hill*, München und Wien 1986, S. 150–157.

[22] GStAPK, Abt. Merseburg, HA Rep. 192 Ritz, B 19, S. 51.

[23] GStAPK, Abt. Merseburg, HA Rep. 192 Ritz, A Nr. 575, S. 13.

[24] GStAPK, Abt. Merseburg, HA Rep. 192 Ritz, B 18, S. 55.

[25] Die hier angedeuten Angaben zur Mythologie und Symbolik des Pfaus sind entnommen aus: Ernst Thomas Reimbold, *Der Pfau*, München 1983.

[26] Gräfin Malve Rothkirch (Hrsg.), *Königin Luise von Preussen. Briefe und Aufzeichnungen 1786–1810*, München 1985, S. 211, 212.

[27] 1804 wurde Albrecht Daniel Thaer auf Betreiben des Staatskanzlers Hardenberg durch Friedrich Wilhelm III. aus Celle nach Preußen berufen; 1806 gründete er in Möglin ein Institut für Landbau. Vgl. dazu: Theodor Fontane, »Möglin«, in: Theodor Fontane, *Wanderungen durch die Mark Brandenburg*, Bd. *Oderland*.

[28] Ferdinand Jühlke, *Die königliche Landesbaumschule und Gärtnerlehranstalt zu Potsdam*, Berlin 1872, S. 22.

[29] Caesar von der Ahé, »Die einstige Rutschbahn auf der Pfaueninsel«, *Mitteilungen des Vereins für die Geschichte Potsdams*, N.F., 1939, Heft 5, S. 426 bis 429.

[30] Marcel Raynal, *Marly 1691. L'escarpolette et la ramasse*, Marly le Roi 1990.

[31] Mehr dazu in: Michael Seiler, »Die Rutschbahn auf der Pfaueninsel«, *Mitteilungen des Vereins für die Geschichte Berlins*, 89. Jg., 1993, Heft 2.

[32] Friedrich Schleiermacher, *Vorlesungen über die Ästhetik*, Berlin 1842, S. 482. Den Hinweis verdanke ich Clemens Alexander Wimmer.

[33] Gustav Adolph Fintelmann, *Wegweiser auf der Pfaueninsel*, Potsdam 1837, kommentiert und herausgegeben von Michael Seiler, Berlin 1986.

[34] Michael Seiler, *Das Palmenhaus auf der Pfaueninsel*, Berlin 1989.

[35] Alexander von Humboldt, *Gesammelte Werke. Kosmos. II. Band*, Cotta, Stuttgart o.J., S. 69, 70.

[36] Gustav Adolph Fintelmann, »Über Anwendung und Behandlung von Blattzierpflanzen und deren Verbindung mit Rankgewächsen für Schmuckgruppen«, *Verhandlungen des Vereins zur Beförderung des Gartenbaus in den königlich preußischen Staaten*, Bd. 10, Berlin 1834, S. 359.

[37] Vgl. Anm. 26.

[38] Zum Thema Maitey: Caesar von der Ahé, »Der Hawaianer auf der Pfaueninsel«, *Potsdamer Jahresschau 1933*, Potsdam 1933, S. 19-31; Anneliese Moore, »Harry Maitey: from Polynesia to Prussia«, *The Hawaiian Journal of History*, Bd. II, 1977, S. 125–161; Wilfried M. Heidemann, »Der Sandwich-Insulaner Maitey von der Pfaueninsel«, *Mitteilungen des Vereins für die Geschichte Berlins*, 80. Jg., 1984, Heft 2, S. 154–172.

[39] Alexandre de Laborde, *Nouveaux jardins de la France*, Paris 1814, S. 99.

[40] Vgl. Anm. 4.

Notes

[1] This is the area according to the survey of 1992. Previous to this, the area had been given as 188 acres (76 hectares). This was based on the lease negotiations with the district of Bornstedt in November 1793. At that time the area was given as approximately 300 Prussian acres = 76 hectares.

[2] Martin Sperlich, »Eine römische Villa an der Havel«, in: Martin Sperlich and Michael Seiler, *Schloß und Park Glienicke*, 3rd impr. edition, Berlin 1987, p .61.

[3] This was the term that the poet and landscape gardener, William Shenstone (1714-1763) used (and coined) with respect to improvements that he undertook on his country estate, The Leasowes.

[4] »For me, the design of a large landscape garden must be based on a fundamental idea. It must be carried out with consistency and if it is to become a tasteful work of art, then as far as possible, one guiding hand should carry the responsibility from beginning to end. This individual may well use the ideas of many others but he alone must intellectually assimilate these ideas, so that the unmistakable stamp of individuality and unity is not lost. I want to emphasize that a fundamental, underlying idea precludes any muddled and random attempts at design. It requires a guiding, continuous concept that can be detected in each individual piece of work. Such an approach might owe it origins to the special characteristics of the artist, his individual background, the earlier history of his family, or to the location itself. It is not at all my expectation, however, that the landscaping be planned down to the smallest detail before work can begin or that the work must entirely conform to such a plan. In a way, I would even recommend exactly the opposite, for although the fundamental idea will define the major features beforehand, while the actual work is being done the artist should be free to react to the inspiration of his imagination and thereby discover much that is new and continue to study his material while it is being created. He must observe the raw nature that lies before him in every possible light, for if it is used well, light is one of his major materials. He must look at his small creation from both inside and outside of its borders and fathom cause and effect. It is only then that he can substantiate his earlier, specific idea for a certain detail. It is also possible, however, that he will have arrived at better insights and will then relinquish part or even all of his earlier idea. From time to time the painter also changes this and that on his painting, and a painting is much less diverse in nature than a garden. He will make a certain positioning more pleasant or natural, improve a shading, impart a feature with more expression. A garden-artist not only works with wilful material that is often very difficult to control, he also has to unite a number of different images into one. How should he be able to do this with complete success on his first attempt!« Hermann Fürst von Pückler-Muskau, *Andeutungen über Landschaftsgärtnerei*, reprint of 1834 edition, Stuttgart 1977, p. 18.

[5] The origins of this name are not clear but almost certainly have nothing to do with the German word for peacock, »Pfau«.

[6] Karl Breuer, *Die Pfaueninsel bei Potsdam*, dissertation Technische Hochschule Berlin, Berlin 1923, pp. 138 to 145.

[7] Ibid, p. 179.

[8] *Voyage autor du monde, par la frégate du roi la Bou-deuse, et la flute l'Étoile; en 1766, 1767, 1768, & 1769*, Paris 1771.

[9] *A voyage towards the South Pole and round the world*, London, 1777.

[10] GStAPK, Abt. Merseburg, Acta des Kabinetts Friedrich Wilhelms II., p. 1.

[11] Carl Christian Horvath, *Potsdams Merkwürdigkeiten beschrieben und durch Plans und Prospekte erläutert*, Potsdam 1798, pp. 222–236.

[12] Hermann Schmitz, *Das Marmorpalais bei Potsdam und das Schlößchen auf der Pfaueninsel*, Berlin 1921.

[13] Bertold Adolf Haase-Faulenorth, *Gräfin Lichtenau*, Berlin 1934, p. 26.

[14] The patent of nobility was issued on 28 April 1796 but back-dated by two years. Ibid, p. 195.

[15] Note 6, pp.36–46.

[16] This connection was first made by Karl Breuer in his dissertation of 1923. Note 6, pp. 148, 149.

[17] SSGP, Sammlung der Inventare, Nr. 393.

[18] Also known as Torre Mesa (Du Pérac 1575), Frontispizio di Nerone or Templum Solis Aureliani.

[19] Georg Forster, *Entdeckungsreise nach Tahiti und in die Südsee 1772–1775*, ed. by Hermann Homann, Berlin 1989, pp. 267, 269.

[20] Cf. note 3.

[21] Cf. Norbert Miller, »Exkurs: Treppenhäuser – Raum als Einbildungskraft des Betrachters«, in: Norbert Miller, *Strawberry Hill*, Munich and Vienna 1986, pp. 150–157.

[22] GStAPK, Abt. Merseburg, HA Rep.192 Ritz, B 19, p. 51.

[23] GStAPK, Abt. Merseburg, HA Rep.192 Ritz, A Nr. 575, p. 13.

[24] GStAPK, Abt. Merseburg, HA Rep.192 Ritz, B 18, p. 55.

[25] This sketch of the peacock's symbolism and mythological functions has been taken from Ernst Thomas Reimbold, *Der Pfau*, Munich 1983.

[26] Gräfin Malve Rothkirch (ed.), *Königin Luise von Preussen. Briefe und Aufzeichnungen 1786–1810*, Munich 1985, pp. 211, 212.

[27] On the advice of the Prime Minister, Hardenberg, Albrecht Daniel Thaer was summoned from Celle to Prussia by Friedrich Wilhelm III in 1804; in 1806 he established an agricultural institute in Möglin. Cf. Theodor Fontane, »Möglin«, in: Theodor Fontane, *Wanderungen durch die Mark Brandenburg*, vol. Oderland.

[28] Ferdinand Jühlke, *Die königliche Landesbaumschule und Gärtnerlehranstalt zu Potsdam*, Berlin 1872, p. 22.

[29] Caesar von der Ahé, »Die einstige Rutschbahn auf der Pfaueninsel«, *Mitteilungen des Vereins für die Geschichte Potsdams*, N.F., 1939, no. 5, pp. 426–429.

[30] Marcel Raynal, *Marly 1691. L'escarpolette et la ramasse*, Marly le Roi 1990.

[31] Discussed in more detail in: Michael Seiler, »Die Rutschbahn auf der Pfaueninsel«, *Mitteilungen des Vereins für die Geschichte Berlins*, 89th year, 1993, no. 2.

[32] Friedrich Schleiermacher, *Vorlesungen über die Ästhetik*, Berlin 1842, p. 482. I would like to thank Clemens Alexander Wimmer for the reference to Schleiermacher.

[33] Gustav Adolph Fintelmann, *Wegweiser auf der Pfaueninsel*, Potsdam 1937, edited and with a commentary by Michael Seiler, Berlin 1986.

[34] Michael Seiler, *Das Palmenhaus auf der Pfaueninsel*, Berlin 1989.

[35] Alexander von Humboldt, *Gesammelte Werke. Kosmos. II. Band*, Cotta, Stuttgart (no date), pp. 69, 70.

[36] Gustav Adolph Fintelmann, »Über Anwendung und Behandlung von Blattzierpflanzen und deren Verbindungmit Rankgewächsen für Schmuckgruppen«, *Verhandlungen des Vereins zur Beförderung des Gartenbaus in den königlich preußischen Staaten*, vol. X, Berlin 1834, p. 359.

[37] Cf. note 26.

[38] On Maitey cf.: Caesar von der Ahé, »Der Hawaianer auf der Pfaueninsel«, *Potsdamer Jahresschau 1933*, Potsdam, 1933, pp. 19–31; Anneliese Moore, »Harry Maitey: from Polynesia to Prussia«, *The Hawaiian Journal of History*, vol. II, 1977, pp.125–161; Wilfried M. Heidemann, »Der Sandwich-Insulaner Maitey von der Pfaueninsel«, *Mitteilungen des Vereins für die Geschichte Berlins*, 80th year, 1984, no. 2, pp. 154–172.

[39] Alexandre de Laborde, *Nouveaux jardins de la France*, Paris 1814, p. 99.

[40] Cf. note 4.

1. Plan der Pfaueninsel im Maßstab 1:4000. Vermessung und Zeichnung von Monika Wahnschaff nach einer Konzeption von Michael Seiler, 1993. Legende:
1 Schloß, 2 Kastellanhaus, 3 Schweizerhaus, 4 Fährhaus, 5 Runder Garten, 6 Holländische Küche, 7 Standort des 1880 abgebrannten Palmenhauses, 8 Palmenhausschuppen, 9 Jakobsbrunnen, 10 Rosengarten, 11 Ergängzungsrosengarten, 12 Fragment der russischen Rutschbahn, 13 Fregattenhafen, 14, Palmen- und Blumenhäuser, 15 Lama-Brunnen = Fragment des Lamahauses, 16 Maschinenhaus, 17 Fontäne, 18 Winterhaus für fremde Vögel, 19 Voliere, 20 Wasservogelteich, 21, Kavalierhaus, 22 ehem. Stallgebäude, 23 Jagdschirm, 24 Gotische Brücke, 25 Portikus oder Luisentempel, 26 Meierei, 27 Kuhstall, 28 Büffelteich, 29 Fähre.

1. Plan of the Pfaueninsel, scale 1:4000. Surveyed and drawn by Monika Wahnschaff after a concept of Michael Seiler, 1993. Key: 1 Castle, 2 Steward's House, 3 Swiss House, 4 Ferry House, 5 Round Garden, 6 Dutch Kitchen, 7 site of the Palm House burnt down in 1880, 8 palm-house shed, 9 Jacob's Well, 10 Rose Garden, 11 Supplementary Rose Garden, 12 fragment of the Llama House, 16 Machine House, 17 Fountain, 18 winter house for exotic birds, 19 Aviary, 20 Waterfowl Pond, 21 Guest House, 22 former stables, 23 Hunting-Box, 24 Gothic Bridge, 25 Porticus or Temple for Queen Luise, 26 Dairy, 27 Cow-Shed, 28 Buffalo Pond, 29 Ferry.

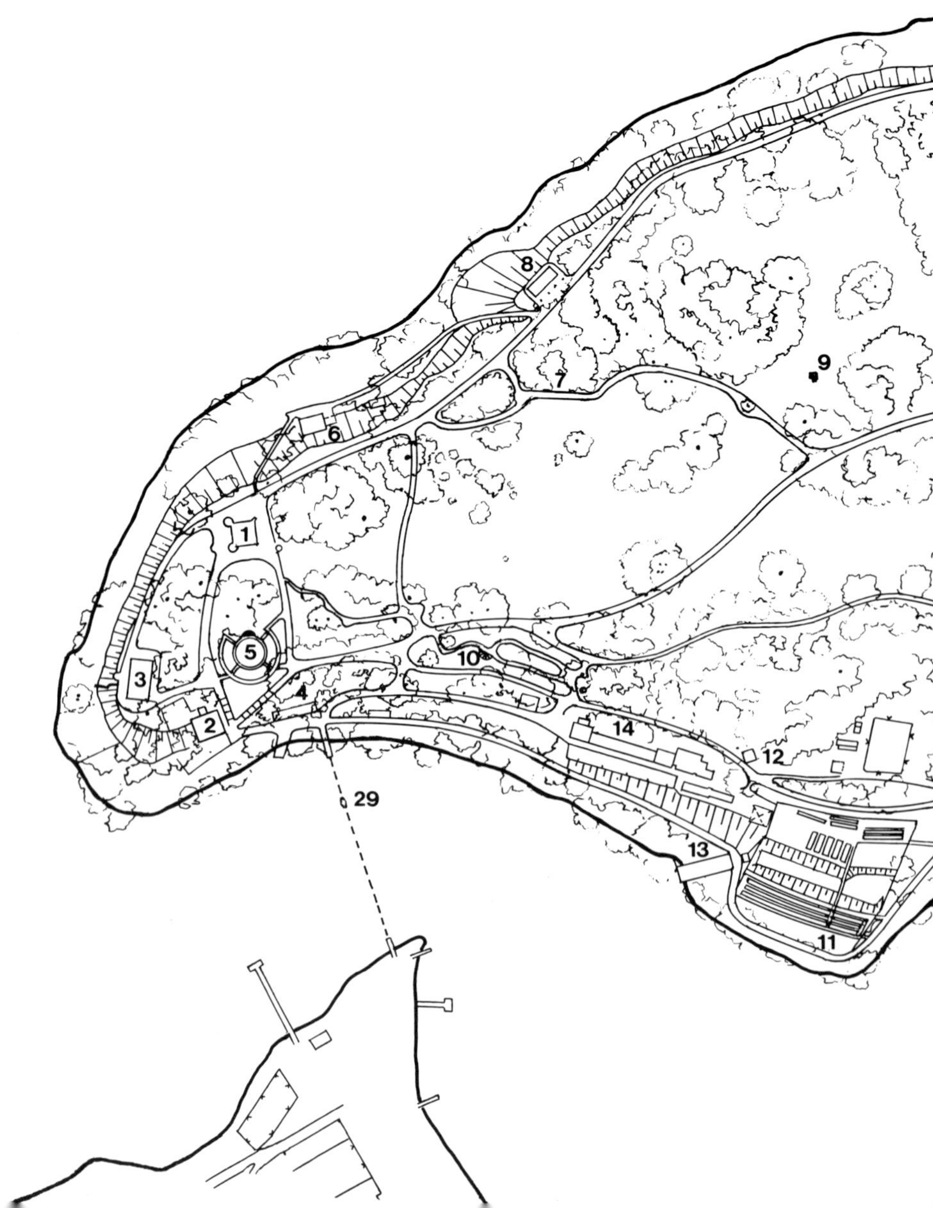

15
16
17
18
19
20
21
22
23
24
25
26
27
28

S. 34/35

S. 34/35
2. Die Pfaueninsel von der Sacrower Spitze aus gesehen. Dem im Boot von Potsdam auf die weißen Doppeltürme des Schlosses Zusteuernden zeigt sich links
hinter der grünen Gehölzmasse zugleich die Schaufassade der ebenfalls in Weiß gehaltenen Meierei.

p. 34/35
2. The Pfaueninsel seen from the Sacrow spit. When
approaching the Castle's two white towers from Potsdam in a boat, one equally sees to the left, behind the
green mass of the forest, the main façade of the Dairy,
which is also painted white.

3. Schweizerhaus, Kastellanhaus, Schloß und Fährhaus
von der landseitigen Fährstelle aus gesehen. Bühnenbildhafte Komposition des Themas Dorf und Burg.
4. Die ehemaligen Palmen- und Blumenhäuser ober-
halb des Südufers der Insel.
5. Der hölzerne Fregattenhafen (1832) von Albert Dietrich Schadow, die »architektonische Wassergrotte«.
6. Das Maschinenhaus, Wohnhaus des legendären
Maschinenmeisters Friedrich. Von hier wird seit 1825
bis zum heutigen Tag das Havelwasser in das Reservoir
der Fontäne gepumpt.

3. Swiss House, Steward's House, Castle, and Ferry
House seen from the ferry station on the other side. A
theatrical composition on the subject of village and
castle.
4. The former palm and flower sheds of the gardeners
above the south shore of the island.
5. The wooden frigate harbour (1832) by Albert Dietrich
Schadow, the »architectonic water grotto«.
6. The machine house where the legendary machinist
Friedrich lived. Since 1825 the water from the Havel River has been pumped from here into the reservoir of the
Fountain.

7. Das Schweizerhaus (1830), von Karl Friedrich Schinkel, das ländliche Urbild griechischer Architektur.
8. Das Kastellanhaus (1796), ein bewußt dörflich konzipiertes Gebäude mit zurückgesetztem Obergeschoß
aus Fachwerk und vielfarbigen Findlingen für Plinthe,
Stützpfeiler und Fensterfaschen.

7. The Swiss House (1830) by Karl Friedrich Schinkel,
the rural prototype of Greek architecture.
8. The Steward's House (1796), which was deliberately
conceived as a house in a rural village, with retracted
half-timbered upper storey and multi-coloured untreated
field stones for plinths, supporting pillars and window
trimmings.

9. Der Bogengang am Kastellanhaus, der vom schlich-
ten Landeplatz zum Runden Garten hinaufführt.
10. Der labyrinthische Rosengarten Lennés aus der
Höhe aufgenommen.
11. Die Blumenkreise des Runden Gartens.

9. The arcade near the Steward's House leading from
the modest landing-stage to the Round Garden.
10. The labyrinthic Rose Garden by Lenné seen from
above.
11. The flower circles of the Round Garden.

12. Das Schloß von Osten.
13. Das Schloß von Westen mit der dem Neuen Garten
zugewandten kulissenhaften Schauseite.

12. The Castle from the east.
13. The Castle from the west with the stage-like main
façade looking towards the Neuer Garten.

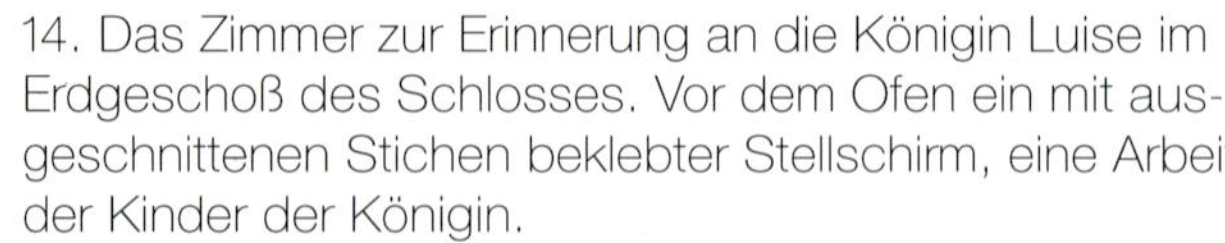

14. Das Zimmer zur Erinnerung an die Königin Luise im Erdgeschoß des Schlosses. Vor dem Ofen ein mit ausgeschnittenen Stichen beklebter Stellschirm, eine Arbeit der Kinder der Königin.

15. Das neben dem Otaheitischen Kabinett liegende Teezimmer im Erdgeschoß des Schlosses mit den 29 allegorischen Gipsreliefs auf Gipsporphyr.

16. Das Otaheitische Kabinett im Erdgeschoß des Schlosses. Die Wandbilder zeigen das Schloß und das Marmorpalais umgeben von tropischer Vegetation. In der Mitte der gemalten Bambushütte hängt eine »milchweiße Glaslampe in Bronze nach griechischer Manier gefaßt«.

14. The room in memory of Queen Luise on the ground storey of the Castle. In front of the stove a movable screen with cut-out engravings by the Queen's children.

15. The tea-room next to the Otaheite Cabinet on the ground storey of the Castle with the 29 allegoric plaster reliefs on plaster porphyry.

16. The Otaheite Cabinet on the ground storey of the Castle. The mural paintings depict the Castle and the Marble Palace in the midst of tropical vegetation. A »milk-white glass lamp set in bronze in the Greek manner« is hanging in the centre of the room.

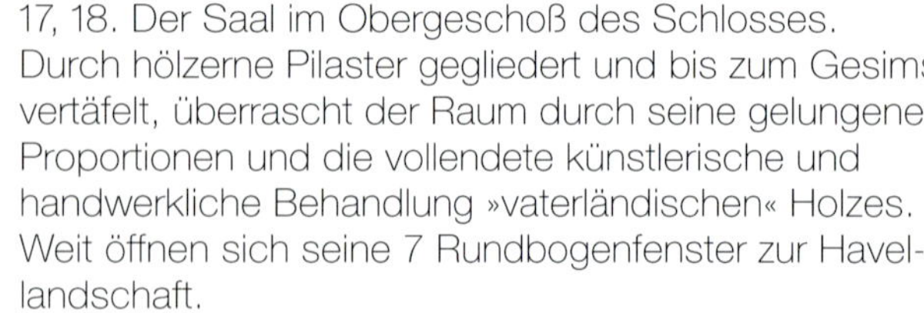

17, 18. Der Saal im Obergeschoß des Schlosses. Durch hölzerne Pilaster gegliedert und bis zum Gesims vertäfelt, überrascht der Raum durch seine gelungenen Proportionen und die vollendete künstlerische und handwerkliche Behandlung »vaterländischen« Holzes. Weit öffnen sich seine 7 Rundbogenfenster zur Havellandschaft.
19. Das Turmzimmer im Obergeschoß des Schlosses. An den Wänden 14 aquarellierte Kupferstiche von Giovanni Volpato mit Ansichten der Vatikanischen Museen.

17, 18. The banqueting hall on the upper storey of the Castle. Articulated by wooden pilasters and panelled up to the moulding, the room comes as a surprise because it is so well-proportioned and exhibits such skilful and artistic use of »fatherland's« wood. The 7 windows with round arches provide an unobstructed view of the landscape of the Havel River.
19. The tower room on the upper storey of the Castle. On the walls are 14 copper engravings with a wash by Giovanni Volpato depicting views of the Vatican Museums.

S. 48, 49
20. Das Schloß von Osten.
21. Die Menagerieachse in Richtung Nordosten. Im Hintergrund der Havelberg.

p. 48, 49
20. The Castle from the east.
21. The Menagerie Axis looking north-east. In the background the Havelberg.

22. Durchblick zur Fontäne vom Mittelweg aus. Mit
außerordentlicher Sensibilität haben Lenné und Fintelmann diesen überreich strömenden Schalenbrunnen
mit der Parkanlage verbunden.
23. Der zweifache »Wassermantel« der von hohen und
dichten Bäumen gerahmten Fontäne rauscht wie ein
Monsunregen, während zugleich der feine Wasserstaub
die Luft belebt und erfrischt.

22. The Fountain seen from the central path. Lenné and
Fintelmann were highly sensitive to the relationship
between the Fountain with its lavish overflow and the
surrounding park.
23. The double »water coat« of the Fountain surrounded by tall and dense trees rustles like a monsoon rainfall, while the fine spray brightens and freshens the air.

24. Der Wasservogelteich mit dem erhaltenen Wasserfall, Teil der ehemaligen Menagerie und Mitte der Menagerieachse.
25. Die Voliere, das einzige erhaltene Gehege der Menagerie.
26. Die Gotische Brücke nahe dem Jagdschirm. Die Brücke wurde 1802 für den Schloßpark Charlottenburg angefertigt und steht seit 1845 auf der Pfaueninsel.

24. The Waterfowl Pond with its preserved waterfall which is a part of the former Menagerie and the centre of the Menagerie Axis.
25. The Aviary, the only part of the Menagerie which still exists today.
26. The Gothic Bridge next to the Hunting-Box. The bridge was made in 1802 for the Charlottenburg Schloßpark and has been on the Pfaueninsel since 1845.

27. Blick auf das Schloß aus der Fontänenachse. Im
Hintergrund die Halbinsel Sacrow.
28. Die »Große Sicht« zur Meierei.

27. View of the Castle from the Fountain Axis. In the
background the Sacrow Peninsula.
28. The »Grand View« looking towards the Dairy.

29. Der Jacobsbrunnen, eine verkleinerte Kopie der schon um 1615 abgetragenen Reste des Serapistempels in Rom.
30. Das Kavalierhaus oder Danziger Haus (1824) von Karl Friedrich Schinkel.
31. Der Luisentempel am Südrand der Laichwiese, dessen Portikus 1829 von Charlottenburg hierher versetzt wurde. Ihrer Bestimmung angemessen, ist die immer schattige Halle nach Norden gerichtet, und die vier dorischen Säulen streift nur zu früher oder später Stunde flüchtiges Sonnenlicht.

29. The Jacob's Well, a reduced copy of the remains of the Serapis Temple in Rome which had already been destroyed around 1615.
30. The Guest House or Danzig House (1824) by Karl Friedrich Schinkel.
31. The Temple for Queen Luise on the southern border of the Spawning Meadow. As befits a temple, it faces north and is always shady; it is only very early or very late in the day that fleeting sunlight touches the four Doric columns.

32. Der 1802 in der Art einer gotischen Kapelle bei der Meierei erbaute Kuhstall, heute Kutscherwohnung und Pferdestall.
33. Die Meierei, die »ein eingefallenes gothisches Gebäude vorstellt«, von Südosten.
34. Die nach Potsdam gerichtete Schauseite der Meierei.

32. The Cow-Shed, built in 1802 next to the Dairy in the manner of a Gothic chapel, today the house of the coachman and also a stable for horses.
33. The Dairy, »representing a ruined Gothic building«, from the south-east.
34. The main façade of the Dairy looking towards Potsdam.

S. 60, 61.
35, 36. Der Gotische Saal in der Meierei. Der Saal ist von einem der ersten Theatermaler seiner Zeit, Bartolomeo Verona, nach einem Entwurf von Michael Philipp Boumann wie ein Bühnenbild für die damals außerordentlich beliebten Ritterstücke in phantasievoller Neugotik ausgemalt worden.

p. 60, 61
35, 36. The Gothic Room in the Dairy. The room was decorated in an imaginative Neo-Gothic style by one the era's pre-eminent painters of stage-sets, Bartolomeo Verona, according to a design of Michael Philipp Boumann; it was done in the manner of a stage set for a play about chivalry, a genre which was extremely popular at this time.

S. 62, 63
37, 38. Fünfhundertjährige Stileichen am Ufer des Par-
schenkessels.

p. 62, 63
37, 38. 500-year-old oaks on the shore of the Par-
schenkessel.

39. St. Peter und Paul auf Nikolskoe mit Durchblick
zum Schloß Pfaueninsel.

39. St. Peter and Paul on Nikolskoe with the Pfaueninsel Castle in the background.